**THE GREATEST FORCE IN THE UNIVERSE
IS THE ONE READING THESE WORDS**

Infinite Being
Awakening your soul through the Law of Reflection

Vaz Sriharan

LCS Books
London College of Spirituality Books

Universal © 2012, Vaz Sriharan, LCS Books

This book has Universal Copyright. This information is given to assist and share. Please use any or all information, to share and evolve. All information belongs to the One Source, You. As you evolve the information you receive, you radiate new truths via your own unique portal of expression, assisting humanity and planet in its evolution. If the author is quoted in the material please ensure the only the exact original words are used in the quotation. Please do not reproduce more than 1,000 words without reference to the author. Please do not reproduce any information to profit from. We appreciate any support you can give through donations.

First Edition, published 2012

Printed in United Kingdom, United States and other countries

ISBN 978-1-4709-6744-4

Also by this author:
Channelled Readings
Meditations, Visualisations & Attunements
- Connecting to your Divine I Am Presence
- Akashic Records: Healing Your Past & Future
- Chakra Balance
- Lyran Star Guide & Galactic Heritage Attunement

To purchase these MP3 meditations, and for Channelled Readings please visit www.londoncollegeofspirituality.co.uk

To learn more about the causes of LCS and Vaz's work, and to donate, please see back of book.

Table of Contents

INTRODUCTION 7

SECTION ONE: KNOW THYSELF
Truth & Awareness 11
Who am I? 15
Consciousness 16
Aspects of our Universe 19
Kaleidoscope Vision 19
The Game of Duality 21
Compassion / Unconditional Love 23
Spiritual Laws of the Universe 27
The Three Minds 35
Energy Awareness 42

SECTION TWO: BEYOND ILLUSION: FEAR & THE EGO
Fear 47
The New Paradigm Ego 53
How do I balance the Ego (how do I heal my fears)? 58
Perceiving Growth in all experiences 60
Learning from experiences 61
Cleansing / Reprogramming our subconscious mind 66
Repairing through Affirmational Healing 68
Repairing through Visualisations 72

SECTION THREE: SOUL LOVE

Equality 79
Your life is a mirror 81
Owning Your Reality 87
Attachments 94
Embracing Your Dark Side 113
Guilt, Jealousy & Envy 132
Learning Forgiveness 137
Transcending Judgement 142
External Conditioning 149
Expressing Yourself 155
Respecting Yourself 170
Creating your Sacred Space 185

SECTION FOUR: INFINITE BEING: LIVING THE LAW OF REFLECTION

The Law of Reflection 197
Purpose & Meaning 202
Destiny 202
Synchronicity, Living the Magic 205
Decisions, Decisions 211
Embracing change 227
Humility 241
Joy, Passion, Playfulness 243
Living in Flow: Letting Go of Control & Surrendering to All That Is 246

INTRODUCTION

Many of us feel as though we are accidents on the planet, bumping into each other randomly, hardly affecting our surroundings. We allow ourselves to believe that we are like a ship on stormy waters, being thrown about by the unpredictable waves of the ocean. We live our lives feeling powerless as we try to adapt to life's uncertainty. We feel isolated and separated as life becomes an upstream struggle of suffering, fear and chaos.

In truth reality is more amazing and complicated than we have allowed ourselves to believe. We are far more connected to our surroundings on a deeply intimate and intricate level. We are both the ship *and* the ocean.

This turns our original philosophy of being at the whim of life's ocean completely around. Instead, we begin to see how we can not only steer the ship in any direction but we also control the very movement of the ocean. We each have the power to control and create our surroundings. It is this realisation that awakens a powerful truth from within. A truth that spirituality has taught from the very beginning - that we have, and always have had, full control of *everything* we experience in life.

This, of course, changes everything. It changes the very nature of how we view reality. We now understand that the ocean is not a separate entity but is in fact an aspect of our greater self.

As we begin to open our eyes fully, we see that the truth has always been prevalent around us. It is present within every aspect of nature, physics, biology and chemistry – all displaying the intricate interconnectedness between all things.

As our awareness grows, so does our quest to find truth, meaning and purpose to our lives. No longer are we at the whim of the ocean – we are no longer fearful and powerless of what happens to us in life. Instead, we realise that we have ultimate sovereign power over everything we experience.

Each of our realities are defined by who we are and what our inner world represents. Perception is everything. Ten observations made of one event will differ for each observer. This is because each observer is perceiving reality relative to his or her own perceptions. Beliefs, loves, fears, opinions, personality, judgments, sensitivity, emotions all converge to form the observer's individual perception of reality.

It is our perceptions that define the reality that we experience – therefore what we are creating. As we resolve our fears, insecurities and limited philosophies, we ensure that these are not reflected in our outer world. Our lives become incredibly enriching, where *anything* is possible – our dreams become our reality.

The whole process of accepting our inherent powers, our interconnection and the true nature of our reality is the acceptance of something far more important for words alone. It is the acknowledgement of the source of all this power. This leaves us with the most profound truth of all. Something that we have attempted to ignore, suppress and deny for aeons but something that can never be quelled.

For the Source of this Power is You.

SECTION ONE
KNOW THYSELF

Before we learn to Live the Law of Reflection, it is crucial we know what we are reflecting! Who are you? What is inside you? What are you made of?

By understanding who we are, which is an ongoing magical journey of self-discovery, we continually understand what we are – and thus reflect this in our outer reality. This is not simply something you are *told* but something you experience through spiritual transformation. This first section serves as a reminder and sets the foundation of what you, and billions of others, have discovered through working through their "stuff" (spiritual growth) – discovering that deep within is an incredible infinite being capable of absolutely anything.

Truth & Awareness

What is Truth?

Our soul holds our deepest Truth and the more we move closer to our Heart Self the more we align our Self with this fundamental and beautiful realisation. It is the journey that evolves us, not the destination. For the destination is and always will be – Home. As we return to our True Self we develop deeper and deeper understandings of Truth. Truths are constantly being redefined as we reach higher and higher levels of awareness. Beliefs that we held so dearly last year seem like those of a stranger to us now. This is the process of Ascension.

Our individual perceptions are what defines our unique Truth. Ten observations made of one event will differ for each observer. This is because each observer is perceiving reality relative to his or her own perceptions. Beliefs, filters, opinions, personality, sensitivity, emotions all converge to form the observer's individual perception of reality. No one Truth is more 'truthful' than another. Truth is like the rays of the sun, each ray reflecting a different expression, yet all linking to the same source – the sun. The sun representing the whole truth.

You are Truth in expression. You represent a ray of Source, expressing your individual Truth. You are perfection in its entirety, each existing to express your individual Truth.

We each have a Truth – a crucial Expression that can be harnessed as a talent or skill to give to the world. We each have something so fundamentally unique that the world is incomplete without it. When we express our Truth to the world, we are fulfilling something that is far greater than our own desires. We are helping to co-create and expand universal consciousness by completing and adding to the Whole.

The Whole Truth is constantly evolving through the interactions of all individual Truths so that it can become more than what it was a moment before. The less rigid belief systems that we hold onto the freer we become, which in turn evolves our personal Truths to access more of the Whole Truth – accessing more of Source.

When we acknowledge that our perceptions create our reality we can then change our reality by changing our perceptions. When we break down old negative, limiting patterns and this will be reflected by our outer reality. We become freer. Freedom is in being truly open to all possibilities.

We also constantly magnetise towards us those that share our own Truths. The more we open up and let go of judgement, the more we move into a whole new arena of discovery. The more we realise that wisdom is in being the ever-inquisitive, ever-learning child, the more we expand our consciousness to whole new levels. Being wise is accepting that we are both the eternal student and the eternal master.

Societally, the old ways have allowed the Truths of the few (governments, institutions and religions) to deem the Truths of the many. The new way allows each of us to speak our own Truth from what we feel is right and allow the Truths of others to act as a reflection. By sharing our Truths we ignite the fire within another to speak their Truth, leading to an ever-expanding worldwide consciousness.

So it is important that we realise that those beliefs and Truths that we hold so dearly onto *now*, may indeed be expanded upon or broken by other Truths in the future. This is not to defy the Truths that we have now, for these Truths are essential to our growth right NOW. Instead it is so we become aware of this process of releasing and embracing so the process of death to our old truths may not be as painful.

The more open we keep our minds, the more we allow the Universe to rain upon us more and more wisdom. As we remain in this state of unknowingness, we gesture to the Universe that we are ready for change. We indicate that we are not afraid of the unknowingness. We are sending a clear sign to the Cosmos and our Higher Selves that we have Faith in the unknowingness, in life.

The more we open up and let go of judgement, the more we move into a whole new arena of discovery. The more we realise that wisdom is in being the ever-inquisitive, ever-learning child, the more we expand our consciousness to whole new levels. Being wise is accepting that we are both the eternal student and the eternal master.

Ultimately we have come to an age where we are becoming more empowered of our Self. We are becoming empowered enough to realise that each and every one of us holds a vital Truth to the whole.

Raising our awareness allows us to access more of the Whole Truth. This is because when we raise our awareness we are seeing our own life from a higher perspective.

When we raise our awareness higher and higher we see beyond the suffering (the dangerous forest) and see that through life's turmoils and troubles can exist limitless abundance. Therefore our Truth is expanded upon and heightened. The more we raise our awareness the more we understand our brother and sister and the more we see of the sun, the Whole Truth.

> You are a Master of your own Truth and
> a student of the whole Truth

We can access more and more of our personal Truth by raising our awareness. The more aware we are, the more we see life for what it really is and the more we can experience.

All Truths can be expanded upon – that is the beauty of spiritual learning. We can zoom in on any aspect we desire and focus our heart's intent on it to draw further Truths or we can sit back and bask in the eternal Truth of existence.

As we each speak our Truth, another will come and bring in a new Truth. We must endeavour to let go of all that which we desperately cling to, based on our fears and learn to embrace the unknowingness that is creation. For example, the Truths written right here will undoubtedly be expanded upon, broken up and heightened by another and another and so forth. Thus is the beauty of co-creation and evolution.

All Truths are an essential part of the Whole. Each of us has an important teaching for the rest of us and each of us has an important lesson to learn. Awareness is ever-expanding and as we constantly attain higher and higher levels of awareness, higher and higher levels of Truths will constantly emerge.

Who am I?

Behind those eyes that reads these words heralds a force so powerful that it can be seen across creation. The power that you harbour is infinite, it exists beyond time and space. It is the same energy that flows through stars, planets and galaxies flows through your very being.

This power is the Source of *everything*, the spirit within every element of known and unknown existence. This infinite power is that of your *consciousness*, the living force within all things in the Universe.

I AM.

This sentence is full in itself. It reflects your supreme power, for you are ALL THAT IS.

You are *all things*.

You are the sun and the moon, the planets and the stars, the trees and the earth, the sky and the oceans.

Everything is energy – the trees, oceans, sky and earth – and you. Energy flows through all things, including you. It is the same energy that vibrates on the smallest molecular level, all energy is irrevocably one.

You are part of your surroundings. Everything around you is an extension of your sacred Self. Energy cannot be destroyed, instead it moves through form. When you die, your energy will continue to be energy just in another form. Energy is infinite. Everything is continuous, therefore you cannot die. You are energy in form, your human body. You are infinite. You are part of the infinite Whole.

Consciousness

Consciousness is the essence of the Universe, it is the Source of All That Is. It is from here, that all things are born, all things die to and all things are reborn.

Your consciousness flows from the Source of *All That Is* – infinite intelligence, infinite power and, of course, infinite Love.

The sacredness of your being is the essence of who you really are. It is the understanding that there is a profound interconnectedness between all things. The nature of interconnectedness is the realisation that everything is inextricably connected and in effect part of a Universal Whole. It is the understanding that everything has consciousness, for everything is in some way a part of the greater Whole.

This greater Whole has many names – Source, Supreme Consciousness, Infinite Intelligence, GOD, the Universe, Life Force, Chi, Spirit, Oneness. The name matters not but what is important is *your* part in the picture. For *all parts* make the greater Whole. All parts including your part.

You are this Source, this Universe, this Chi, this GOD, this Life Force, this Oneness.

The Oneness is *in* all things. The Oneness *pervades* all things. The Oneness *is* all things. You are this Oneness. You are GOD.

Imagine, if you will, the Oneness / Creator / GOD / Source representing all the energy in the Universe, *All That Is*, in the form of a gigantic mirror. Now envisage this mirror shattering into infinite pieces, each piece a reflection of another. You are one of those pieces, a reflection of the Oneness, an eternal spark of Source exploring your Divinity.

You are an aspect of the whole– the whole Universe – yet this does not deny the aspect that you are. There is no measurement to your Divinity, for you are infinite. You are a Divine spark of creation, each as powerful as your heavenly brother and sister. You are Divinity expressing itself in countless, magnificent ways.

You complete the Whole, for the Whole is incomplete without you. Existence needs each and every single being. You cannot be replaced. If you go missing, everything and everyone in the Universe – the plants, trees, animals, stars, planets and all the Beings - will notice your absence. They *cannot* exist without you. Everything is inextricably linked. Such is the sacredness of your Being and the interconnectedness of all things.

You are the divine masculine and the sacred feminine. You are both, you are all. You are the GOD and the GODDESS. You are Divinity in form. You are the form disguising itself as the formless. You are the unlimited unmanifest potential.

You are a Divine Spiritual Being experiencing a Human Existence. You are this *infinite* nonphysical force that cannot truly be separated, playing a game of *finite* illusion in physical form.

It is time to remember your heritage, as an eternal being of Light.

You are an eternal diamond. The illusion of fear, created by the illusion of separation, is simply the dirt on the face of the diamond. It is time to clean off the dirt and see the magical being that you really are.

LOVE

The Oneness is the Source of Unconditional Love. This Source is the infinite reservoir of pure Love, from where all is created and blossoms. You , by your very nature, are pure Unconditional Love. You are Love in physical form.

As will be discovered, everything comes back to Love. That is because everything comes out of Love. The key to existence, is Love.

Who are you? Why are you here? Why would a soul who seemingly has infinite knowledge at its foundation level be here to experience and know itself? Why would the Oneness experience itself in this way?

Only you can know the true answers to these questions a- and as you explore yourself, you will be amazed at what is stored deep within you. For you hold the treasures of truth that you have experienced over this life and others.

Now is the time for these truths to be accessed and expressed to expand Universal Consciousness

Aspects of our Universe

There are many aspects of our Universe that are integral to existence on this plane. As these teachings have yet to be discovered or accepted by traditional education, we find ourselves lost and disconnected in this world, unsure of the reality and the extent of our powers.

Kaleidoscope Vision

> Everything is perception. The world around you is a complex flux of realities – digested by your own consciousness through your own set of filters, ultimately giving you your unique reality. Everything you see in the world is processed through these filters painting a picture of *your world*.

All our beliefs, opinions, judgements, loves, hates, desires, wants all converge to filter what see in the world – giving us each a unique vision of the world. One way of understanding this is by imagining your vision as that of a kaleidoscope – where your vision is effectively distorted by your own personal perceptions of the world. Consequently, it is your perception that distorts reality and gives you your own special picture of what is happening. In the truest sense, no one sees the true reality – we all see our own version of reality.

This is crucial for it allows us to understand reality on a much deeper level as well as of course finally understanding the reality before us. All of your filters work towards processing what you see – these have been in place since the very moment you entered the world and began processing what you experienced. Everything you learned about life – through your environment, parents, family, friends all change your perception of what life is.

For example, ten observations made of one event will differ for each observer. This is because each observer is perceiving reality relative to his or her own filters – his or her own perceptions. We each have a different perception of what the world looks like and what is occurring in the world. Of course when we look at commonalities such as a chair or the sky, we can all describe it basically the same – but even then, the way we describe it, its usage and its meaning to us is very different. When we move into the arena of perceiving the world, we are each very different in our vision.

The Kaleidoscope vision is a beautiful testament to the variety of truth and of us all on this planet. However, we must recognise that kaleidoscope within us if we are to truly understand ourselves and others. This is because the kaleidoscope only gives us our own unique vision of reality. In order to understand others, and therefore ourselves, we must endeavour to access more of reality.

Let us take the example of a farmer who lives on the bottom of a valley. He looks after his crops and often becomes agitated as he does not know whether the rains will come. His vision of life is limited. However, a farmer who manages his crops at the top of the valley, on the hills, can see until the horizon. He can see far in advance whether the rains will come. His vision is greater than that of the farmer on the valley floor; his awareness is greater than that of his counterpart.

It is compassion that clears our kaleidoscope vision and allows us to see more of reality. It is compassion that allows us to work through our own filters in order to access more of the truth, to see more of reality. As we discover more of reality, we discover more about ourselves – because of course we are working through our filters but also we are understanding more – we are raising our awareness to that of the farmer on the hills.

THE GAME OF DUALITY

Physical existence is an experience of duality.

Our entire reality is a reflection of this. Male and Female. You have two arms, two legs, two eyes, two halves of your brain, two kidneys, two lungs. Right and Wrong. Left or Right. Positive and Negative. The Sun and the Moon. The Day and Night. Our entire reality is a testament to duality. And duality has been the basis of our entire existence. It is understanding duality that allows us to transcend it, which is what we are being asked to do, to reach our natural state of Oneness. It is this state that we are actually free to move through reality without judgment and limitation. Freedom is Happiness.

Duality divides and separates by its very nature, dividing every situation into two sides. This effectively polarises everything we see and do into two sides, Light and Dark. The Light represents what we see in life as good and positive, whilst the Dark represents what we see in life as bad and negative.

As part of our Earth experience, we naturally polarise towards one end or the other – we feel we must embrace the Light to feel good, positive and happy or we embrace the Dark and feel negative and dwell on our heavy emotions.

However, transcending duality requires us to see the value in both – it is the middle-ground, the balance of these two aspects of Divinity. While it may be relatively easy to see the 'good' benefits of the Light, it can be difficult to see value in the Dark.

The Dark is merely an absence of Light. When you turn a light on in a dark room, what happens? The light transmutes all the darkness into light, it permeates everywhere. The dark does not hide in a corner and try to overcome the light! The Dark has no power over the Light. This is the true nature of Light, for it transmutes and refines everything it touches. The Dark is simply where love (light) has yet to reach. The Dark is by definition limitation, fear and ignorance, whereas the Light represents understanding, wisdom and love.

The Dark provides the space for our Soul to permeate, to explore and expand into. It is not something to be feared, it is something that heralds an infinite arena of exploration. The Dark provides the space for learning, it provides us with the challenges that allow us as souls to spiritually grow. The Dark is an essential part of us, for it *is* us – we are All That Is.

Therefore, those who polarise purely to the Light are ignoring a crucial part of themselves by not exploring the Dark, and vice versa. By focusing purely on our 'good' attributes, those feelings that make us feel happy, we are denying a fundamental aspect of our-Self. The Dark, while heralding pain and suffering, holds intrinsic value for exploring. It provides the space for Self-discovery. The Dark is just a part of us as is the Light. It is how we *approach* the Darkness that defines us. This is explored in much greater detail later in this book.

When we see value in our challenges in life, we grow – and this process is reflected by Compassion.

Compassion / Unconditional Love

Compassion is the most powerful force in the Universe.

Compassion is the middle-ground between the Light and the Dark. It is the realisation that there is value in *both* poles of Divinity. Compassion sees the spiritual growth value in the Dark as well as the uplifting effects of the Light. Compassion allows us to seek and appreciate the balance between whilst simultaneously being non-judgemental of those who polarise to either side. Ultimately, compassion takes us to a place where we are allowing of both our-Self and others in the embodiment of Unconditional Love.

Compassion sees all situations from a higher perspective, observing the intrinsic value of an event from all angles. Ultimately this means seeing the short term and long term benefits that can be extracted from a particular event. While, in the short term a painful event may herald anguish and suffering, it is compassion that allows us to see the long term benefit of spiritual growth, wisdom and understanding.

A child is a wonderful example of how torn we are between protection and compassion. For a child to grow and learn in this world, we know that mistakes must be endured so that the child realises *why* this is not the way. It is through the mistakes that we all learn. So by offering the child our loving support we help them overcome these challenges – this is compassion.

However, if we protected our children every time they were hurt and attempted to shield them from any pain or suffering whatsoever, we are denying them crucial learning opportunities to further their growth and wisdom. If we use pity and sympathy as a form of love, we are not truly offering them all the freedom that they as Gods and Goddesses themselves deserve. We are denying them the ability to reason and evaluate by themselves about the nature of the world, thus limiting their growth and future happiness. Ultimately we are claiming their life for our own. Compassion sees the truth in true love – unconditional love – and ultimately seeks the highest good of all.

We are all children and are continuously learning and growing. We can look at ourselves in the same way that we look at a child, learning its way through the Universe.

Unconditional Love is the highest, purest form of energy. It is the acceptance and allowance of all others' energy and Truths as well as that of your own.

Unconditional Love is the embodiment of compassion.

Unconditional Love allows us to be at peace with who we are, where we are and what is happening around us. It needs not conditions for us to Love and therefore we cannot be harmed by externalities.

When we love another with conditions, we are coming from a fear-fuelled power-driven desire. This is where our love is determined by certain aspects of another's behaviour. If this other person fails to meet these conditions then our love for them is challenged. Unconditional love places no conditions on the love given and asks for nothing in return.

A common misconception is that unconditional love means unconditional allowing. People often assume that unconditional love means putting up with conditions regardless of how one feel about them. However, this line of thinking denies the Self – a crucial aspect of the Whole! Unconditional loving is to love yourself *and* others simultaneously. Unconditional love is the act of allowing yourself to express in your own unique way and allowing for others to uniquely express themselves concurrently. If something is not to your liking in another person then allow them their expression of being and turn your attention elsewhere. It is the very embodiment of non-judgment, for it is in this state that we allow for the boundaries of others as well as our own. It is the knowing that all expressions of Truth are part of the Whole. Others' truths may not particularly resonate with you but you can allow them to express it while honouring your own Truth. What resonates deep within *you* is what is important for *you*. If it is aligned with your highest intentions then it will be for the greatest good of all. Remember no one's Truth is 'better' than another's, they are all flavours of the Universal Truth. However, what *is* important is your *own* Truth.

Unconditional Love allows us to be safe in the truth of who we are – once we are happy with ourselves we can do anything we want. It also allows us to love another unconditionally for all that *they* are. If you feel that someone is attempting to control you, then compassionately speak your Truth. This, itself, is an act of Unconditional Love. For here, you are expressing your being and are helping the other to realise that they may have control issues.

Unconditional Love is a balance of your wants/needs and that of another. This is why it is essential to work on yourself and establish what and who You are, so that you can learn to love yourself unconditionally first. Only then can you go out into the world and love another in equal measure. Otherwise the feelings of love often become clouded by insecurities and power games.

Whilst many of us can experience unconditional love for others, such as our child or parent or pet, most people find it difficult to mirror this unconditional love to themselves. The inner child within you is your eternal child. Learn to see yourself in this way and you will begin to love your-Self in a much more deeply enriching way.

This form of love for one-Self opens doors to the limitless possibilities and abundance that are always available to you and that you always deserve. When you begin to love yourself unconditionally, you open the door to the God(dess) within you. Whilst this may seem to be a daunting experience, where do I start? It all begins with awareness. Once you make a step on the journey, your Spirit will take over, and lead you the way.

Spiritual Laws of the Universe
The Law of Free Will

> **The Law of Free Will**
> In all matters there is total free will. You have the free choice to create, feel and do anything in your life.

You are in *total* control of your reality. Every decision you make, every action you take, every experience you embrace is born out of your own personal choices. It is the ultimate playground.

You have total choice how you feel every single moment – this simple fact is actually one that is never taught or acknowledged. You have total free will to create anything you desire – a life of pain, misery and limitation or one of joy, abundance and exploration. You choose.

This is the essence of free will/free choice, so that we choose to spiritually evolve. We choose our experiences. We choose how we react and experience our experiences. The choice is yours.

The Law of Manifestation

> **The Law of Manifestation**
> Your Thoughts Create Your Reality. Your inner state of being dictates your outer reality.

As perfect reflections of Source Creator, you have been blessed with all the powers of creation. You may not know it but everything you experience in this world is purely a reflection of your thought & feelings.

Your subconscious mind writes the script for your outer reality, based on the thoughts that you pass onto it.

Even through our pursuit of science we have already determined that everything is a form of energy: Einstein's $E=MC^2$ states that energy equals mass times the square root of the speed of light. Therefore mass is a *form* of energy.

Physical matter is simply energy vibrating at a very slow speed. As we move up from dense matter to sound and then to light, we see that energy gathers its pace and vibrates faster and faster. The higher frequencies of energy represent thought, where our emotions also lie. Our thoughts are coupled with our intentions and pass through these levels to form into matter, thus creating our outer physical reality.

So as the energetic Beings that we are, our thoughts play the crucial role in what we experience. For in essence you are pure Consciousness, pure Energy dreaming. Everything around you is a projection of your thoughts, your dream.

Everything you do, every word that you say carries your energy – it is sent out into the Universe for Manifestation. The Universe is beyond duality and therefore holds no judgement of what you think. It will manifest impartially, be the thought positive or negative.

The Law of Manifestation works in harmony with the Law of Attraction and the Law of Reflection.

THE LAW OF ATTRACTION

> **The Law of Attraction**
> Whatever you *feel* is magnetised to you in physical form. Your inner state of being writes the script of your outer reality.

The Law of Attraction and the Law of Reflection are both really one law, however they have been separated here to better illustrate their mechanisms within this Universe.

Your life is very symbolic of a movie – you are the writer, director, actor and reviewer of this movie. All other parts played by friends, family and loved ones are attracted to your movie through your scripting – in other words through the Law of Attraction.

So whatever thought you harbour will be manifested into reality, and those that reflect your thoughts will be pulled into your movie. If, for example, you feel that you are a victim in life then you attract people who victimise others. If you are highly self-critical, then you may very well attract those who will similarly criticise you. The more we focus on negative aspects in our life, or that which we are lacking, then the more we will attract this in our outside world. This is essential to our learning – so that we may become aware of the world outside to become aware of the world within. Once we do and we learn to love ourselves, then we will attract those who love us similarly. You see the beauty of this law once we align our Love with it? When we are *in* Love with ourselves and others, then we attract Love and loving people to our reality.

The Law of Attraction works in harmony with the Law of Reflection and the Law of Manifestation.

THE LAW OF REFLECTION

> **The Law of Reflection**
> Your outer world is a mirror of what is occurring within. Your relationship with yourself is reflected in your relationship with your world.

Our external world is a simply a mirror of our internal world. This beautifully constructed reality allows us to see in our outside physical world what is actually happening to us on the inside.

Your relationships with people, situations, experiences is a reflection of your relationship with your-Self.

The purpose of this law is to help us learn what is happening within. So when we are reflected by those around us, we can effectively see *who we are*.

If we feel unhappy and insecure, this will be reflected by the people and situations we find ourselves in. If for example you feel that no one listens to what you say, then this may be a reflection that you are not listening to yourself. Similarly, when we are fully content with our-Self, then the universal Law of Reflection will mirror this in our outer reality.

The Law of Reflection works in harmony with the Law of Attraction. Whatever we feel on the inside is *attracted* to us in our outside world. Existing people or situations are brought into our reality that already mirror our feelings. *The Law of Reflection works in harmony with the Law of Manifestation* – whatever we feel on the inside is manifested into our reality on the outside, we *manifest* situations based on our internal fears or our internal love.

THE LAW OF REBIRTH

> **The Law of Rebirth**
> All life (energy) on this plane moves through three cycles: Life, Death, Rebirth. It is also symbolic within all experiences on a microcosmic scale.

Reincarnation was once believed to be an act of punishment, where "good" deeds in one life would be rewarded by a "good" life in another, and inversely. Reincarnation is so much more and actually relates to an incredibly complex beautiful system that allows for continued spiritual growth, exploration and creativity.

In essence, it is one of the reasons for this plane, this reality we all experience and the lives we lead. Through a continual cycle of birth, death and rebirth – a soul may learn over time and space – a depth of self-understanding unparalleled when compared to a single life.

This cycle also represents the cycles that we all go through. Everything has a cycle. Nature is our ultimate teacher. Spring, Summer, Autumn, Winter. This represent the life, death and rebirth cycle of life. The trees do not cry at death, they understand its powerful, sacred purpose. The trees understand there is no true death, only a process of letting go – so that the new, the spring, can emerge with a beauty of its own. Understanding this cycle is key to our journey. We have trouble letting go due to our belief that we are finite. In truth, there is always a spring waiting for you, around the corner.

The Law of Karma
(Cause & Effect)

> **The Law of Karma (Cause & Effect)**
> Your outer world is a mirror of what is occurring within. Your relationship with yourself is reflected in your relationship with your world.

The purpose of Karma (Cause & Effect) is so that we may learn our life's lessons, so that we may become wiser as souls and ultimately evolve.

The Law of Cause & Effect can be resembled to the analogy of dropping a pebble into a pond -creating ripples and waves throughout the water. Everything you do has a consequence. Every thought, word, desire creates ripples throughout the Universe.

Any discomfort in our lives is a direct result of our own manifestations. Yes this may be from another life, yet it is time we looked at *all* our lives as one long life. When we do this we see that karma is really just a reference to the Universal Law of Attraction. What we put out, returns to us. There is no judgement on behalf of the Universe, instead it is a way of re-balancing energy.

This is a brilliant system by the Universe of nudging us on the path of spiritual growth, away from pain, and towards slowly understanding that Love is the answer.

However, more often than not it is the *process* of cause &effect that is so often misconstrued.

Karma is not simply 'an eye for an eye'. As Gandhi pointed out, "An eye for an eye will leave everyone blind."

Karma is extremely intricate and correlates to the particular evolution of the soul involved. For example, if a child makes a mistake then it would be inconceivable for that child to be lessened to the same extent that an adult would be. There is a distinct learning process for that child and so there will be a distinct reaction (effect) that will return to that child to further its growth.

BEYOND KARMA

Karma is not punishment. It is a way of learning how we are making choices that are not desirable for our own state of being and how our choices affect others. It is a method of displaying to us what is in harmony with Love and what isn't. For you are Love, and when we act out of our own alignment, it is a method of revealing to us what is out of alignment. When we make negative choices that affect ourselves and others, we are informed in the form of the *effect* so that we may understand the consequences of our actions. Thus we are being taught by the Universe how to realign ourselves with our true Divinity and learn to love ourselves.

We have reached a stage in our evolution where we can actually transcend karma, move beyond cause & effect, if we understand its purpose. To repay karmic debts, we can transmute the experience into a much more pleasant one by offering to be a student of what this karmic issue (or situation) has to teach us. When we begin to take the knowledge and wisdom from every situation and see every moment as part of our growth we begin to transcend the arena of cause & effect. This is because we instantly recognise the lesson to be learned and thus the whole purpose of Karma is negated - we do not need to experience the effect to learn the wisdom for we already understand it! *Awareness* is the key to transcending karma.

So really, for our purposes in this age, we can move beyond the Law of Karma and concentrate on the Laws of Reflection and Attraction. This brings us crucially back to the present. This allows us to have a greater understanding of what we are doing and how our thoughts and actions are affecting both us and those around us. It is being in a state of awareness where one realises all experiences are for growth, in one way or another.

The Three Minds

Subconscious, Conscious and Superconscious Minds

Whilst labels and separation are illusions in themselves, they can offer us further insight into ourselves providing we are not defined by their parameters. Thus we are offered even further and deeper spiritual growth. The human mind can be, and has been, defined as being composed of three types of consciousness – The Subconscious, Conscious and Superconscious. Each of these consciousnesses reflect an arena for our Spirit to utilise for an array of possibilities on the physical plane. Also each of these consciousnesses represent an aspect of our whole Self.

Remember, your mind is not in your head! Instead the physical body is *in* your mind.

Subconscious Mind

The Subconscious mind is subservient to the Conscious mind. It operates at a basic, instinctive level and has no powers of reason. It is totally impartial to whatever enters it and reacts immediately to whatever it is told.

The Subconscious mind is an extremely powerful consciousness. It is infinite.

The Subconscious mind is responsible for creating our reality. All thoughts from our Conscious mind are passed on to the Subconscious and manifested into reality. The subconscious takes our thoughts and marries them with our intentions to manifest into physical matter. The Subconscious mind also works in harmony with the Law of Attraction – everything that the Subconscious mind believes it will attract. If you live in fear you will attract fearful situations *and* create more fearful situations on your part.

When we experience painful or loving situations it is the very nature of our *beliefs* set in the Subconscious mind that is creating these scenarios.

The subconscious mind is constantly conditioned by our beliefs and experiences about our reality. Much of what the subconscious mind knows is conditioned very early on in childhood and adolescence. Our parents, environment, loving and painful situations during our early years cause us to theorise how the world works. These sets of beliefs are stored within the subconscious mind and are carried into adulthood creating a narrow but effective view of the world before us. However, we can easily become slaves to these beliefs and the choices we make throughout life reflect the pains that we experience as we grow up.

Let us take an example and look at a young boy, who is raised by particularly over-protective parents. This boy, Johnny, grows up with the premise that the outside world is dangerous. He is not allowed to go out with his friends to play and his fearful parents ensure that he is kept away from other parents and strangers at all times. As Johnny grows up, he formulates theories within his subconscious mind that others are not to be trusted. Johnny's parents' over protection creates fear-based theories within. This coupled with the fact that he will constantly manifest protective or smothering people in his life through the Law of Attraction, means that this man will be trapped in a cycle of pain.

So we can see the effect of this fear-based belief within the subconscious mind has had on this soul's freedom. Fear-based thoughts and feelings pass down from the Conscious mind to form sets of fear-based beliefs (insecurities) within the subconscious mind. These insecurities then manifest into reality as well as dictating the choices we make in our daily lives.

The key to breaking the patterns that our subconscious mind repeats is to first heal and cleanse the subconscious mind through purification. This cleansing basically involves acknowledging and understanding our pain, dealing with it and repairing the damage so that we move up and outwards. Repairing the damage requires reprogramming the subconscious mind with loving-based beliefs. Affirmations and visualisations are processes that reprogram the Subconscious mind to re-condition it with a new set of beliefs (repairing the damage so to speak). Why live in fear, suffering and pain when you can fully experience the rich limitless abundance that is readily available? Simple examples of conditioning the subconscious mind is learning to drive a car – once we have learnt this process, it is stored within the subconscious mind so that we do not need to learn it again.

We have for so long allowed the subconscious to dominate our conscious mind. However, if we learn to utilise the power held within our subconscious minds, we can achieve anything we desire. The subconscious mind holds the key to unlimited abundance. By healing the pains and sufferings held within it, we can transform the reality that we create and experience. By reprogramming the subconscious mind, we can instil new sets of light, loving beliefs that will change the way we make conscious decisions. More significantly, it will transform our manifestations into that which we desire.

The Subconscious mind is also responsible for our dreams and this is one of the ways that we can tap into what our sets of beliefs and ultimately our insecurities, actually are. Dreams are a form of feedback to the Conscious mind so that we can be aware of what is actually happening within our subconscious. This is because we are largely unaware of why we are creating such situations and are often unaware of how rigid our beliefs actually are. Pay attention to your dreams and they will provide you with yet another way of understanding what is really happening within you. Just by acknowledging an insecurity that you have experienced within your dream will help bring it to the surface to alleviate it. Awareness is, as always, the key.

The subconscious mind is also responsible for our physical well-being. When we see physical problems emerge in our body, it is a direct result of the subconscious mind's manifestation. Thoughts of self-hatred, victimisation and bitterness are passed onto the subconscious mind, which reacts accordingly. Self-hatred, which is a self-destructive belief, will inform the subconscious mind that you want to be destroyed and this where diseases can be manifested.

The key to attracting abundance, Love and Light to our lives is by lovingly empowering and reconditioning the subconscious mind with loving, positive sets of beliefs. This is done by turning the tables so that our Conscious mind is the Master of our Subconscious mind.

CONSCIOUS MIND

The Conscious mind is designed to master the Subconscious mind and be subservient to the Superconscious mind.

Much of our problems lie in the fact that we allow our Subconscious mind to control our Conscious mind. Sets of beliefs formed during childhood and adolescence are grounded in the subconscious mind and these affect our decision-making abilities in the present moment. This leads to a limited world of possibilities as we allow past events to dictate our present and future ones, for fear of being hurt again in the same way. Instead we should be striving to live in each moment as if new. A child is a perfect example of one who does not allow their Subconscious mind to control them. Each and every moment is a new day, a new beginning, a new moment of existence that they can freely do anything they desire. A child's Subconscious mind is subservient to their conscious mind (which is in turn subservient to their Superconscious mind). Thus, they see life as it should be – magnificently abundant and excitingly unpredictable.

When we allow the Subconscious mind to control us, we strive for security and predictable events so that we may not be hurt.

By embracing life from the Conscious mind, we can choose to live in love and create anything we desire.

The Conscious mind is the only mind that does not have a direct link to the un-seen energies of the Universe. This is the very nature of our being here on Earth, so that we may hone our abilities to effectively use all three minds to connect with Source and raise our vibrational frequency.

SUPERCONSCIOUS MIND & THE INFINITE SELF

The Superconscious mind represents the doorway to the Infinite Self or the Infinite Divine Self. When we access the superconscious mind, it is also the eternal Divine – the arena of the infinite unknown. It is the arena from which inspiration and imagination is sourced. It is the sacred limitless potential. The unmanifest. By tapping into this mind we can access the infinite wisdom, love and abundance that is readily available to us all.

We don't always realise what or why things happen to us. Our Infinite Self holds the knowledge that we have gained from all our lives – past, present and future. Whilst the subconscious mind (soul) also holds this information, the key difference is that the Infinite Self knows all. The Infinite Self is connected to the Whole, where all knowledge and all wisdom dwells. Therefore, our Infinite Self is our True Self in our natural form. Our subconscious mind represents the learning centre that we aim to inspire with the teachings of our Infinite Self. When we align ourselves with our highest intentions, we are synchronising ourselves with what we came to Earth to do, teach and achieve.

The point in aligning ourselves with our Infinite Self is so that we can align ourselves with our true infinite Divine essence. Our Infinite Self knows what is best for us and knows our heart's desires. By choosing the philosophies of our Infinite Self over that of fear-based philosophies (effectively our Ego), we allow ourselves greater scope for achieving abundance. The Infinite Self knows all, it has the sight of an eagle and sees even beyond the horizons. It sees past the challenges that we face and sees the rewards on the other side of the hills.

Whilst the above can explain in logical formula the role of our Infinite Self, this merely dwarfs the true relationship we have with our Infinite Self. Your Infinite Self is your best friend and confidant. The love your Infinite Self holds for you is beyond any words known in our language. If you imagine for a moment how you feel when you are alone, you might feel like there is no one there to comfort you and no one to understand your pains and sufferings.

Now imagine that you have an inextricable bond with a best friend, be them male or female. This best friend is unlike any you have ever encountered, you can tell them anything for you trust them implicitly. They know *everything* about you, yet do not judge any of it. You know they love you completely and wholly, they would do absolutely anything for you.

Now imagine that everything you feel, they feel. All the times you laugh and play, they laugh and play. Every time you become excited and joyful, they too rejoice with you. Now consider this, every time you feel alone and desolated, your best friend feels this pain too. All the turmoils, pains and loneliness you feel is mirrored by your best friend who cries with you, desperate to make you feel better. This best friend is your Infinite Self. You are inextricably linked with your Infinite Self, who does not, cannot and will not leave your side for any instant. Your Infinite Self will not infringe on your free will and so can only watch and gently nudge you along your path throughout your life so that you can achieve greater happiness, joy and abundance.

Using your own free will and awareness you can make contact with your Infinite Self and move into that space that is in effect You. Your Infinite Self speaks in the wordless language of the Heart. Listen to the song of your Spirit and let the melody guide you to yourself.

Energy Awareness

Everything is energy, in one form or another. The physical body is simply the densest part of our auric field. The aura encompasses our consciousness on Earth. As we move from the outskirts of our aura towards our centre, the energy fields become denser until they climax to become the physical body.

We each have the ability to sense energy and use this ability whether we are consciously aware of it or not. As energetic beings, we all send out and receive energy continuously. As you think over the events of yesterday, today or tomorrow you use a process called visualisation. Through this process, your state of being radiates energy into the Universe, reflecting yourself and by Law of Attraction you magnetise what you put out.

We are all capable of picking up energy in others – this intuition about another's emotional state goes beyond simply assessing how they feel. On a subconscious level, we are hearing their true thoughts and react accordingly. The saying 'you could cut the atmosphere in here with a knife' is a good example of how we pick up energy. When we enter a room where there has just been an intense argument, we pick up on the negative energy. By its very nature, negative energy is thick and heavy – a very low vibration. When one feels negative, they emanate vibes that will attract people who think similarly or feel similarly about themselves.

Similarly, when one feels love and happiness they will attract people who feel the same. The saying 'a smile is infectious' is very true and so 'an inner smile is infectious' – positive vibes will spread like wildfire when you radiate love and warmth within you. Those who see the world as a fearful, depressing place will naturally attract both fearful and depressing people and situations. This is because the Law of Attraction directly attracts the energy we send out.

Energetic vibes embalm every thought we have, be they positive or negative.

The very moment you think of another being, you send out an energy impulse that hits their auric field. If this thought is loving and positive it will heal and honour that being as well as attract more lovingness to *your* life. If the thought is negative and hateful then it will negatively affect that being's auric field and will also affect you by attracting negative and hateful people into your life. There are many ways we can improve our 'radar' of sensing energy but one of the most effective ways is to be still and know our *own* energy first. Then as we become used to what is ours, we will immediately notice the energy of another. Luckily, this is one aspect that many people are very good at already. Many of us notice when there is negative energy in a room or when someone is feeling particularly down. Similarly, we all notice how positivity spreads like a raging fire, lifting the spirits of all those it encounters. Laughter is undoubtedly one of the most infectious forms of energy.

As well as being surrounded by energy, we are constantly being sent guidance from our Infinite Self and guides from the higher realms of existence, the varying dimensional levels. Our world is rich with little nudges from above to show us a brighter way to go. We have all experienced strong miracles in our lives through these little nudges, however over time we allow our Ego to put it down to coincidences. There is no such thing as a coincidence – it is a small or large miracle from the Universe sending us a clear message.

Psychic abilities range over a wonderful assortment of our extra-sensory talents. Clairaudience (inner hearing), clairsentience (inner feeling) and clairvoyance (inner seeing) being among the most common known forms of accessing energy.

Psychics are more generally known today as 'sensitives', reflecting their sensitivity to energy. This is an excellent way of reflecting a better understanding all our abilities. We are all sensitive to energy and to other people's emotions and this is what psychics are adept at – being able to open their sensitivity further to allow in a greater deal of energy for their inner senses to read.

We can all learn to tap into these abilities. Believe in yourself. By raising your awareness of yourself, you will open up to the wonders of the Universe.

Awareness is a state of mind and the ability to see things from a new higher perspective.

SECTION TWO
BEYOND ILLUSION
FEAR & THE EGO

It is time to re-evaluate how we look at things; how we look at *everything*. Fear and The Ego have been taught in many ways over the millennia and most of these ways teach us to separate ourselves from them. But what if these concepts are not what we think?

Fear

Polarity divides our nature into love and fear. It is often thought that hate is the opposite of love, however fear is love's true polar opposite.

Fear is present throughout our lives. If we look at the way we think, the way we act, the way we limit ourselves – we see that fear is a concurrent theme.

Without even realising, fear is always playing a part in our lives. Our stresses, our judgements, insecurities, limitations emerge from a place of fear. We have become so conditioned to fear that we have accepted its place in our daily experience. But what is fear?

Our problems arise from our external and internal conditioning with regard to fearful philosophies. Fear itself is a philosophy, one that serves to limit, withdraw, segregate, compare. The philosophy of fear creates a hierarchy, where we are on a ladder – here there will always be another to make us feel inferior and we will feel it necessary to find others to feel superior than. However, fear is much more than this.

From our very early childhood, we begin to process the world and begin to incorporate fear into our lives. Our subconscious mind is conditioned by our external experiences through our environment and creates theories upon the world – be they positive or negative. Our family environment, friends, schools, institutions, society – all play a part in creating a picture of the world that is then painted by the subconscious mind – in order to create stability for ourselves. This allows the subconscious mind to formulate what it thinks the world is like – so that we may effectively live in it.

Let us take an example and look at a girl who grows up under the heavily critical eye of a parent. Now Sarah may enter the world as an adult perceiving everyone as being potentially critical of her behaviour. During childhood, her subconscious reacted to being heavily criticised by creating the theory, "I will be criticised by others." Consequently, Sarah becomes wary of others to avoid further pain. As Sarah moves through adolescence and adulthood, she enters the world with her pre-conditioned belief that people are critical. She interacts with others in some cases by pre-empting a possible future pain where they might attack her (much like her own parents did) by criticising them first. This pattern of behaviour undoubtedly closes her off from fully expressing herself, for fear of being criticised. This coupled with the fact that she will constantly manifest critical people in her life through the Law of Attraction, means that this woman will be trapped in a cycle of pain.

Let us examine this more closely. What has occurred here? Sarah's early childhood has been conditioned by the criticism she received from her parent. This criticism is basically taken on as negative conditioning i.e. fear-based reasoning. The criticism that Sarah receives is obviously harmful, however we are not blaming the parent here for they have their own reasons and path that has led them to their predicament. Instead we focus on Sarah. So her subconscious mind receives this negative conditioning by formulating negative theories on the world (insecurities). These insecurities are created in order to pre-empt possible future pain by basically painting a picture of what the world 'must' be like based on current experience. However, what we must note here is that the subconscious is using fear to base its philosophy.

Let us look at these fear-based beliefs, these insecurities that Sarah has created and see how they have and are affecting her life. Sarah's inner belief that others are bound to attack or criticise her has limited her in serious ways. It prevents Sarah from fully embracing any relationship without first fearing what this other may want, how they may judge her and how they may possibly hurt her. Her past experiences and *ultimately how she reacted to these experiences* has led Sarah to create barriers to protect herself from pain. These barriers are essentially her insecurities and although are first created for protection are in fact the source of her pain!

So what does Sarah do? As Sarah recognises that her pain is a result of her own choices – where she recognises that she has created her own barriers and only she has the key to release herself from her prison, can she be set free. Fear limits, it holds us back, it makes us defend, offend, retract. Fear destroys – that is its nature.

When we align ourself to fear-based philosophies i.e. negative conditionings (insecurities), we give our power away. We have effectively limited our world and of course our happiness. In this example, we see that Sarah has created large problems for herself in her outer reality. Through her intimate relationships, friendships and also her confidence in general – have all been affected by how she perceives the world. Through her kaleidoscope vision, she sees the world as a critical place where others judge you, where others are better than you and where you are inferior. This has left her consistently on the defence and offence – a place that will always be stressful for everyone is an enemy, especially yourself!

As Sarah brings a new philosophy into her life, she liberates herself from her shackles. She doesn't allow her past to dictate her present and future. This is the philosophy of Love

THE REALITY OF LOVE

Fear represents a place where we do not understand the whole picture. From our place of ignorance, we naturally act and react negatively because our philosophy is limited. Fear results in a feeling of being threatened in some form or another. When we do not love ourselves i.e. when we are not secure, we fear (we are insecure). These insecurities are effectively parts of our-Self that have yet to be blessed with the Light of wisdom. It is Compassion (the embodiment of unconditional love) that allows us to see the whole picture. Compassion can also allow us to see that our kaleidoscope vision of this other reflects an aspect within ourselves.

Ultimately, fear represents the insecurities within us – the parts of ourselves that are in pain that require love. And this is ultimately what fear is.

Fear is an illusion

Fear represents the parts of ourselves that are in pain, the parts that lash out in a defensive manner, the parts that make us withdraw. Our fearful parts are essentially the parts of ourself that have been ignored, suppressed, neglected. These parts do not simply vanish! Just like children, these parts of us rebel – they emanate in all parts of our life through our projections, manifestations and thoughts (the Laws of Reflection, Attraction & Manifestation). Just like abused children, these parts of ourselves are traumatised – from being neglected from ourself! And just like children, there is one primary solution towards healing – Love.

Love is the source of all knowledge and all wisdom. It is the reservoir of creation, exploration and limitlessness. Love allows us to grow. As we love the parts of ourselves that are in pain, we are healing them and releasing them from the illusion of fear. Ultimately, we recognise that fear is simply a place where love has yet to reach – it is a staging ground for the parts of ourselves that are blinded by ignorance, that do not know any better. By allowing these parts of ourselves to remain in this state, we seriously inhibit our lives by allowing these insecurities to negatively project and manifest.

When we align our philosophies with the ideology of Love, we are not simply being kind or allowing – we are breaking free of old modalities that keep us stagnated.

When we use love, we perceive all our life experiences as positive – as beneficial in some way or another. This is crucial for it defines how we live in the present. If we look back at this example and look at Sarah, we see that her past experience of being criticised has defined her life experience, albeit a negative one. However, if Sarah uses love and understanding she may recognise that her parent had his or her own reasons for being so critical – maybe they were heavily criticised themselves? Remember that all pain projected is pain felt within. People only hurt others because there is pain felt within.

So returning to our original example, Sarah may see that maybe her experience of being criticised actually has the potential to help her as opposed to be so detrimental. Although the actual experience in her past was painful, maybe she can heal it by taking something positive out of it. Maybe the criticism she felt allowed her to become more compassionate of those who are also criticised, maybe it has allowed herself to explore herself because of the consistent introspection that criticism makes us do? There are many reasons and many ways where positive benefits can emerge yet they can only emerge when we have released the pain and are willing to accept that there may be something positive in this or that experience. When we start to view all our experiences as something beneficial, we release fear and embrace love.

Now that we recognise that fear is an illusion, we no longer have to give it our power. Our fearful parts represent messages to ourselves informing us that these parts require our love!

In order to truly understand the nature of fear and how and why we take it on in our lives, it is helpful to examine one of the most historically vilified parts of our-Self – the Ego.

The New Paradigm Ego

The Earth is a playground for infinite beings to experience finite existence under a veil of forgetfulness. Since an infinite being cannot in reality live finitely, the physical plane of existence serves as an illusion – a dream, created where GOD-the-infinite can experience life as GOD-the-finite.

The Ego represents GOD-the-finite, the physical manifestation of Spirit. It is the physical part of your Divine Self.

The Ego's base belief is that each and every being is separate. This principle allows the Ego to uphold, and believe itself, the illusion that GOD is finite.

By experiencing separation (that which we are not through our Ego), we suffer. As we learn and understand what that suffering means, we come closer to understanding that which we are (our True Divine Infinite Self). This process is spiritual enlightenment / growth.

As a result of being finite, with a beginning and an end, the Ego naturally believes that there is a limited amount of everything in the world. The Ego believes the world is plagued by scarcity. What has been called The Inner Self (GOD-the-infinite), on the other hand, holds knowledge of the infinite and interconnected nature of all things and therefore knows the world is rich with limitless abundance.

The Ego's beliefs are born out of its illusion of finite existence. In this respect the Ego believes that we each have a limited amount of happiness and that we must secure our happiness or increase our happiness from externalities. The Ego believes therefore that we have to *look outside* to be happy, meaning that we source our power externally – through other people, places, situations.

As we can see the Ego uses fear as its primary philosophy. This is because the Ego is ultimately ignorant – it is ignorant of the true reality. Fear represents ignorance and this is why the Ego and Fear walk hand in hand. *Ignorance is simply a place where wisdom has yet to reach.*

Consequently, the Ego's **power struggle** theory is formed immediately upon entering the physical plane. The Ego stipulates that out of every situation, there is a winner and a loser. Even in loving relationships, an untamed Ego will ensure that its recipient is always the winner of any argument or any situation where power is involved. The most apparent problem with this philosophy is that it leaves someone feeling dejected and someone else feeling temporarily uplifted at the expense of another. It is temporary until they find their next 'fix' of power and since their power is based on externalities, it is therefore subject to change. Spirituality, which is aligned with the philosophies of our Infinite Self, tells us that there is a **win/win** outcome to *every* situation, since true infinite power lies within us, something that can never change.

Let us take an example and take a look at a couple, where one partner decides to end the relationship. The fear-based beliefs within us inform us that if we have not made that final decision ourselves then we are the rejected and the other is the winner. This inevitably leads to an immense power loss from the individual as they unwittingly give away their power to the other person. Spirituality (the philosophies of our True Infinite Self), on the other hand, teaches us that there is a winner to every single situation. Every single person has something to teach another when they interact – **Every Master is another's student** and vice versa.

Our Infinite Self informs us that we can take the wisdom that we have been gifted from any experience and now move on with much greater awareness and knowledge than we ever had before. So in this example, the person who felt rejected can now look at the situation and change their perceptions to cater for a more positive reality. They may see that the experience has actually made them stronger as it has reflected an insecurity within them that needed healing anyway. The lesson may be to hold on to their power more. By exploring the positive aspects from this situation, we can see that this person can actually emerge from this scenario stronger and wiser than the one who ended the relationship. This is the essence of the saying "if it doesn't kill you, it makes you stronger." There is much to be learned from loss as well as gain.

Our untamed Ego tells us to feel guilty, jealous, angry, inferior, superior – all because of its base belief that we are separate. It believes we have to source our power externally in order to make up for the scarcity in the world. Its belief that we are separate and finite blinds it to the fact that we can source infinite power from within ourselves. It also blinds it to the fact that love is more powerful and beneficial than fear. When you truly accept the interconnectedness of all, you realise that not only is it irrational to gain power from outside but that you are home to a power far greater than you could possibly imagine. You are All That Is.

Once we connect deep within ourselves we can access all the power we ever need and an infinite times more than we can manipulate from another being. By listening to the philosophies of our True Self, we align with the infinite possibilities that are available and our freedom blossoms. Ultimately, when we are happy with what we have ourselves, then anything that happens around us cannot hurt us in anyway.

As soon as we love ourselves internally and are happy, our external world mirrors this state of being through the Laws of Attraction and Reflection. This is where our abundance lies.

We can now see how our Ego can seriously limit our manifestations and our path to limitless abundance.

However, remember that we are here to balance and love *all* aspects of our Self, for we are All That Is.

In this respect, it is time we re-evaluate how we view *everything*.

RE-EVALUATING THE EGO

If we see our Ego as something we need to suppress or ignore then in reality we are ignoring a part of ourselves, a crucial part of ourselves for that matter. This is because The Ego is a part of us! It is the Divine physical representation of our Greater Self! So it is time to re-evaluate how we view the Ego and challenge its historic perception.

Consequently, we realise that our Ego is a hurt and pained part of us, like a child. When each soul incarnates, it enters a world rich with diversity and opportunity. Yet this plane also heralds suffering. As an individual grows up in this world and experiences the pains and sufferings of childhood, adolescence and adulthood, they form sets of beliefs and barriers to protect themselves against harm. This process, well documented in psychology, is necessary and instinctive for a person's subconscious mind to form these beliefs, theories and barriers to avoid future pain. This is in effect the Ego (GOD-the-finite) reacting to the outside world (or the Ego forming itself). Our Ego responds to the situations it is faced and reacts by developing barriers and beliefs. Sufferings that we endure during childhood and adolescence define the sets of beliefs, theories and barriers that the subconscious mind develops and holds onto. The Ego responds to the pains that we experience using an instinctive survival-based drive to ensure that we do not re-experience that same pain. This process is essential for ensuring our survival. It is very similar to putting an innocent child into a rough neighbourhood and telling him/her to grow up on their own. The child grows up very quickly by learning from its experiences and 'staying out of trouble' by avoiding similar experiences. This is essential for the child's survival.

This is a metaphor of our relationship with our Ego. The rough neighbourhood is very similar to the Earth plane and here we realise:

The Ego is our Inner Child!

Our Inner Child, on faced with physical reality, responds to the situations it is faced with and formulates a series of theories and beliefs. It is essential that these beliefs and theories are formulated near the beginning, to protect us from emotional and physical pain. The beliefs and theories are generally fear-based because of societal and parental conditioning as well as the Ego/Inner Child's base belief of separation.

With this new perspective, we can now see that the Ego and the Inner Child are exactly the same! They are interchangeable, for they both represent GOD-the-finite. It is duality that makes them seem separate to us. They are polar opposites of each other, so in reality they are the one and the same. By healing our Ego we allow it to merge with the Inner Child and we have our Ego/Inner Child balanced.

So now we can view our Ego in a completely different light. As we begin to see our Ego as our Inner Child in pain, we understand its trauma. The Ego reflects the Inner Child's Dark side, its shadow. Therefore, we use Light and compassion to heal it.

So, in reality, we are healing ourselves! By re-evaluating the Ego, we better understand how crucial it is for us to love all parts of ourselves. You recognise how vitally important it is to treat your-self well, as a child – to nurture and love and respect. These parts of you in pain and require your love and attention. As you heal your Ego, you balance your Ego/Inner Child and are therefore healing yourself. *Love all parts of your-Self.*

How do I balance the Ego (how do I heal my fears)?

What does this all teach us?

It teaches us that fear is an illusion. It also tells us that our Ego is a part of us, it is our Inner Child in pain.

So what was the point in differentiating them? It teaches us to love our Self in a much more connected way by seeing the Ego as a part of us. If we simply thought of our fears as something that we must 'get rid of' then we are still failing to see what this fear is. This fear isn't simply a part of you that you need to release, it is a part of you in pain – a part that hasn't yet reached the Light. This is an exciting time for this part of you! For when it does reach the Light, a powerful transformation occurs and that so-called failing or negative part of you becomes a tremendous asset – it becomes a strength.

To heal our Ego we have to first accept and acknowledge the messages that it is trying to send us. Suppressing the Ego or ignoring or blaming it does not serve us any good, for this only suppresses, blames and ignores a part of ourSelves.

So we first move into an arena where we are looking at our Ego as a hurt child. It is our *Inner* Child in pain. So how do we heal this child?

The Ego presents to us our own fears and insecurities, which we can choose to ignore or heal. By using compassion to heal our pain we are effectively healing the Dark (our fears and insecurities) with our Light. We are en-Light-ening our Selves.

By bringing Light into all areas of our lives, we are exploring. We are expanding ourselves into the limitless unmanifested potential that is the Dark. We are bringing Love to all areas of our lives and by doing so we are expanding creation. For Love expands, creates and multiplies by its very nature just as fear decays, limits and confines.

A hurt Ego naturally formulates its own theories on how to deal with pain – it tells us never to go near that type of situation again! The Ego believes in fear. The Ego believes that fear actually protects us. This is because the Ego's philosophies are flawed. It's base belief of separation allows it to have such credence in the ability of fear to protect. The Ego believes that by being scared of things, we will ensure that we do not get hurt. By cowering, we will not risk being pained. However, through the Laws of Attraction, Reflection and Manifestation, what we ignore is only reflected and attracted into our outer world. Our pain is constantly manifested in our reality until we learn the lesson and forgo it. Hence the paradox of fear.

So to heal our Ego we first disallow the Ego in our discussions! We begin to use our Infinite Self to teach us what is really going on. Psychologically, we are using our Superconscious Mind to teach our Conscious Mind, which in turn teaches our Subconscious Mind. Essentially, we are using all three minds to achieve growth. Spiritual growth is the process of healing the pains and sufferings of our Lower Self (the subconscious mind) with the Light and philosophies of our Infinite Self (the superconscious mind) through the medium of the Self (the conscious mind). And so we become whole, where the we live through the Infinite Self – we have anchored Spirit on the physical plane – we are a Master of Our Reality.

PERCEIVING GROWTH IN ALL EXPERIENCES

As we use our angel eyes, we see the purpose of all experiences with the light of love. We begin to look at our fears and insecurities not as failings but as incredible opportunities for soul growth. The more we think from a level of unconditional love and compassion, the more we shine through our diamond core to reveal our True Infinite Divine Self.

Therefore, healing the Ego means that we recondition what the Ego believes about reality. We effectively teach the Ego about the true reality, about infinite abundance, love and happiness. As we do this, we are of course teaching ourselves. Our Ego/Inner Child heals and we subsequently live more positive lives as we receive constant positive nudges from our Inner Child to grow, expand, be confident and express.

Once we have acknowledged the pain within us we can move on to the next step of actually healing the issue.

There are many ways in our lives in which we allow our fears to control us. There are many incidents in our past where we have allowed our fears to define how we should live. By raising our awareness we can see the cause of each of our fears and then bring light into that part of our-Self to allow us even greater abundance and happiness. Fear just represents a part of our-Self that needs love. Therefore when we use our awareness to transmute that fear, we are bringing more and more love into our-Self – we are loving all parts of our Self.

As we heal our subconscious mind, we enlighten our being and are able to let go of old negative, limiting patterns of thought which ultimately restrict our happiness. The more free, open and loving our thoughts the more we are able to embrace the limitless abundance that is available to us all.

Healing ourselves is a two-part process. First we take the knowledge to be learned from the situation and then we repair the damage. We use our awareness to learn from the situation and then we use our conscious mind to repair the damage within our subconscious mind.

Part One
Learning from our Experiences

The Buddha said, 'Learning is suffering', so ask yourself – what have you learned from your suffering? To begin, we first accept that all our "suffering" has given us a wealth of knowledge for the present NOW. It is essential that we see all our experiences, positive or negative, in Light. All experiences serve us.

How we view bumps along our path is crucial to how we move beyond them. If we view them as obstacles then they will indeed become obstacles. If we view them as challenges to be overcome then we are opening up our world view and not being limited by fear. We see the challenges as something that will help us grow and move us to a new level of understanding.

We all get trapped in vicious circles of pain. Our very nature as loving explorative souls will recreate dramas of pain so that we can move beyond it – this is one of the reasons for the Law of Attraction. Our Ego tells us that everything is a power struggle and that there is only a win/lose outcome to every situation. We believe that we need to draw energy from outside of us. Spirituality teaches that there is a win/win outcome to *every* situation – where no-one is wronged or can be wronged by another. When we allow fear from past events to rule our present and future decisions, we seriously detriment our own freedom.

When you experience a painful situation, the first thing to do is to take a step back and pull yourself out of the scenario. Raise your awareness up, above the situation and look at the situation from a subjective perspective. It is very easy to get sucked in by overpowering emotions that come with an intense situation. It is crucial that we do not allow the emotion to consume us.

Next, take a look at the situation. What happened? Usually we will state that someone was to blame – either yourself or the other person (or situation) involved. It is an instinctive response to protect our personal power due to our philosophy of fear. However, we must realise that no one is to blame. Blame serves no one any good, *especially* you. If we feel like we have made a mistake then we take the knowledge from the situation and thank ourselves for surfacing it to be healed.

Always remember that pain is only triggered by another when there is already pain within you (and vice versa). Pain is simply a place where Love has not yet reached because pain is simply a cry out for Love! So by bringing it out either in yourself or another, you have been done a tremendous favour – you have been shown a part of your-Self that needs Love, a part that needs healing. This is not to say that we should inflict pain on ourselves or others in order to grow! This is instead a way of moving beyond the pain that we already harbour, the struggles that we undoubtedly encounter during our lives. This pain might have been the cause of a multitude of insecurities that have limited you in so many ways. By bringing it out you have given yourself the opportunity for growth and awarded yourself with the door to even greater freedom and abundance.

Painful situations will continuously be repeated until we get it! It is method of making the unconscious conscious. Repetitive dramas unfold as a way of teaching us what is happening within. It is the Laws of Reflection, Attraction and Manifestation working their magic to present to us in our physical reality what is happening within. Once we finally understand the lesson (which takes many of us ample time!) we process it for the last time as we recognise what is occurring. One example is of a woman who continually attracts men who abuse her. Each one is more severe than the last yet she doesn't realise how she is attracting them because each seems to be a completely different character from the other. Of course, her inner world is manifesting her outer world and until she recognises that a deep insecurity of her victimhood is being played out then she will continue to relive the lesson until it becomes conscious.

There are many insecurities that limit us directly through fear, which are then manifested through our subconscious mind. Our subconscious mind eavesdrops on all our thoughts, and all our insecurities, creating the world that it sees fit based on these assumptions.

To dissolve fear we need to face it and see what it is offering us – it is a message that there is a part within us that needs healing and evolving. Writing down your fears is an excellent way of challenging them. We often think we are dealing with our fears when we replay them over and over in our minds, but we are simply allowing our Ego and our emotions to be involved in the discussions. This is a one-sided debate! To challenge our fears we must look at them from a different perspective, one that is not clouded by overwhelming emotional attachments. Ultimately, it involves changing the way we perceive our so-called mistakes.

Perception is everything and our subconscious mind reacts accordingly to the way we perceive things. When we focus on habits we have that we would like to erase, we only attract more of the same by the Law of Attraction! Instead we must change our perspective to be of one of compassion and understanding. When we see the habit as something that we can learn from, we see it already changed and thus we inform our subconscious mind that we do not dislike a part of our Self. We see that part of our-Self as needing love and we love that part of our-Self for showing us an area that requires Light. As we begin to love all parts of our Self, the subconscious mind reacts accordingly and attracts and manifests love into our lives.

Whilst much of our fears and insecurities are formulated through childhood and adolescence, the way we heal these pains is through consciously seeing how they affect us in the NOW. By acknowledging a fear within us we need not see the root of when it was formulated but we see instead how it affects us in the present. Journeying back to childhood years to deal with a problem can be very time consuming and confusing. Instead we can understand that fear is an illusion and see what that fear is teaching us in the NOW to deal with it effectively. This is because the NOW is all that exists – our past is malleable to our present perceptions.

Remember, your Ego may try to see spiritual evolution as a structured incline where you achieve happiness and gradually become happier and happier forever. However, spiritual growth is much more complex than a simple uphill incline of happiness. This is because we are cleansing a multitude of problems within us and there is no order to how they emerge in our lives. Change is always occurring. The Ego doesn't like change because change represents instability and the Ego cannot find security in instability. Spiritual evolution is more often than not 'three steps forward and one step back'. But know that you *are* moving forward! The one step back provides you with yet another opportunity to fully resolve your issues. That stride is getting you closer and closer to enlightenment and being whole.

This shouldn't be a daunting process. The key is to remain in your stillness throughout any tumultuous changes that occur around you – and these changes will become less and less severe the more you grow. *You will reach a point where you do not need to suffer to learn.* Instead you see what has occurred in your life and you use awareness to spontaneously rectify and grow from the situation.

If we are to reach that state of happiness that we so desire, then it is essential for us to take responsibility for our pain in order to move beyond it. It is important that we do not confuse blame with responsibility. Blame is an Ego-based concept that lies one party at fault for a situation. Responsibility means acknowledging that the pain we feel is there because it has surfaced from within us. Responsibility means meeting a situation with a response, which every situation has: Response - ability. Every situation is an opportunity for us to respond in whatever way we choose, be it one of more pain and suffering or one of love and growth.

Primarily to release pain we have to acknowledge that it exists in the first place. Denial is more common than we think. The Ego perceives it as weak to admit to our Conscious Selves that we are in pain. Yet this just creates more pain. Fear of pain breeds more pain. Like attracts Like. Too many times we deny what we experience and this allows these experiences to multiply and grow. When we acknowledge and say to ourselves "OK, I feel pain" then we allow ourselves the opportunity for growth and freedom.

So as soon as we empower ourselves with Light, we heal and balance our Ego/Inner Child. The Ego/Inner Child then begins to work for us as we effectively anchor Spirit in physical form and align it with our Divine infinite Self.

The next section – Soul Love delves into the various ways in which we disempower ourselves through our lack of Self-love. Once we understand the root of our problem then we can bring it the surface and heal it with our wisdom. This is the beauty of awareness, its very touch is healing.

Part Two
Cleansing / Reprogramming our Subconscious Mind

The second part of this process can be split into two – cleansing and reprogramming.

Reprogramming our subconscious mind requires re-teaching ourselves new patterns, conditioning. This is because we have all been taught throughout our entire lives external conditioning and predominantly fear-based programming. The mind does not know the difference between imagination and reality. So we have to effectively un-learn the negativity and sets of limiting beliefs that we have drummed into our poor Subconscious minds and replace it with Light, Loving, expansive thoughts.

Channelling Love

We are free to choose what we embrace in our lives. This choice has always been ours yet we seem to forget this most of the time.

Every single moment, we choose whether we want to experience love and happiness or fear and suffering. Each moment, we decide whether we want to hold onto loving thoughts that enter our field or to deflect negative thoughts that come our way. Our thoughts are passed from our conscious mind onto our subconscious mind.

Therefore it is up to us to be the gatekeeper at the conscious mind to check the thoughts that enter the subconscious mind. The more we consciously watch over what we think about and hold onto, the more we can learn to send only loving, positive thoughts onto our subconscious mind.

This is channelling love. By switching our channel to our Infinite Self we allow our subconscious mind to wake up from the dream of negativity and limitation to the reality of love and infinite abundance. The subconscious mind is very much like a robot, it is impartial and will listen to whatever we tell it to do. However, most of us allow our fears and insecurities to dominate and control our thoughts, therefore constructing many limiting sets of beliefs within the subconscious for manifestation. Take a step back and think how many times you berate yourself for doing things in your life – this builds up a belief in the subconscious that you are worthless and unloved, thus creating your outer reality. Also these thoughts of worthlessness will create patterns of thoughts and reasoning within the subconscious mind, which then affect your actions and decisions – therefore limiting your world. Throughout our life we are sending powerful messages to our subconscious, which paints a picture of who we are and what we experience.

Of course we cannot control every thought that enters our mind! What we can do instead is to begin a process – a new method of thinking. By becoming more and more aware of our thoughts and consciously attempting to set side the negative thoughts, we begin to slowly eradicate these types of thoughts from our vocabulary! In essence, we are retraining the mind and eventually you will see less and less of these types of thoughts at all!

The subconscious mind is very adept at learning new sets of beliefs through practice – learning to ride a bicycle is one such set of programming that is inbuilt into the subconscious mind. After a short time of practice, our subconscious mind will have new sets of beliefs and our conscious mind will not have to work so hard to deflect negative thoughts. It will become second nature to think positively and fearlessly.

By practising this it will soon become second nature for your subconscious mind.

Channelling Love, however, does not mean we control everything about our thoughts so that only positive ones enter. It is not about control. It is about awareness of what is entering our field. For example, we may have passing self-attacking thoughts. Here, we refrain from fully immersing our-Self in this negative thought and instead deflect it. However, we obviously need to deal with where this thought emanated from. (See Embracing Your Dark Side for explanations and exercises in encountering our dark emotions and thoughts).

Channelling Love is a process where we train ourselves to start being aware of our thoughts so that we may gradually allow in and emphasise only positive ones. It is here, where we recognise how these positive thoughts ultimately serve us.

Repairing through Affirmational Healing

As we work towards deflecting negative thoughts, we are faced with the damage already inflicted on our subconscious mind. This is where positive thinking – affirmations come in.

Affirmations are used to re-condition our subconscious minds with Light, Loving thoughts that will serve us to greater freedom. It is a way of healing our fears and insecurities within our subconscious mind with love. The subconscious mind has many old, outdated, negative, limiting sets of beliefs. Whilst, using our awareness helps us see the cause of the problem so that we can transcend it, we need to also heal the damage that we have made within the subconscious mind.

While, we may feel silly repeating affirmations to ourselves, we are undertaking a crucial psychological step in re-conditioning the subconscious mind with more expansive, freeing thoughts. This is because we are constantly sending affirmations or denouncements to our subconscious, whether we realise it or not! Throughout our childhood and adolescence we conditioned our subconscious minds with many sets of beliefs, based on our outer reality and experiences. These beliefs were more often than not fear-based because they were influenced by our Ego and our painful experiences. Through our Ego, we will naturally protect our-Self from emotional harm by formulating fear-based philosophies. Our mission is to overcome these fears using the light of our awareness.

If we think to ourselves, we can see that much of the time we worry about events, people, attachments and these often lead to self-attacking thoughts. These act as the opposite of affirmations but are still passed onto the subconscious mind for Manifestation and Attraction. We seem to have no problem in reciting denouncements to ourselves but have very little time to condition ourselves with affirmations!

Let us take an example:

How many times have you said sentences like "Oh I wish I was like him or her" to yourself? A statement like this sends two clear messages to our subconscious:

1. We are not like that other person, therefore we empower the belief that they are better than us. This ultimately empowers an inferiority complex within us, which affects our present decisions and the way we interact with people.
2. We manifest an outer reality where we actually *are* inferior – because the subconscious knows no better. It will manifest whatever it is told. People on the outside who reflect this belief will then be pulled into this illusion (through the Law of Attraction) and see yourself as inferior. Ultimately, you will surround yourself with people who make you feel inferior.

Do you see the vicious circle here? Why energise self-attacking thoughts when you can live in abundance and joy.

If we take the multitude of attitudes that we have – they are usually a result of years of conditioning from childhood, adolescence and adulthood. We experience a bad situation and tell our subconscious mind "OK, I don't want to experience that again, here's my theory - let's stay away from these situations so that I don't get hurt again" or "this is how people are, let's form a judgement of myself and others and then protect myself by closing down." This conditioning filters down to the subconscious mind (which remember, is totally impartial) and proceeds in manifesting a reality for us based on that fear.

Let us take another example. If we assume that people are going to criticise us due to a childhood shrouded by overly critical parents, then we limit our expression as we close up in the fear that we may be under attack at any moment. Then by the Law of Attraction, we will attract what we fear (always attracting critical people) until we learn the lesson and transmute it into Light. Being angry with our parents or whoever installed this conditioning is irrelevant and will only bring you more pain through bitterness. For what they have given you is a tremendous gift in terms of spiritual growth – if you are willing to learn the lesson of their conditioning then you are one step closer to learning true compassion. Now when you encounter critical people, you can help them from this space.

Affirmations, therefore are a crucial tool in reprogramming our subconscious mind. We want to tell our subconscious mind that we desire to create a better reality for us, a reality where we are abundant and free to express and meet whoever we desire. A reality where we are able to explore our own divinity in the way that we deserve to. We all have fantasies of what we'd like to be, personality-wise – the truth is that you can BE all that, because you have access to any facets that you chose to explore – it is only fear that tells us that we cannot take risks this way.

Affirmations are very much like going back to school, we need to effectively un-learn all the negative programming that conditioned us when we were a child by replacing it with the essential knowledge of Love – the eternal expanding wisdom of Light.

USING AFFIRMATIONS

The vocabulary you use is much more powerful than you realise. You energise whatever you say and it is subsequently passed onto the subconscious mind for processing and manifestation.

What goes hand in hand with affirmations (detailed later in Creating Your Reality) is the crucial importance of intention (through feeling). In order for your affirmation to work and believed by yourself is if you *feel* what you are saying.

As is well known, the most self-fulfilling sentence in our language is "I AM". This is because this sentence reflects everything that you are – I am pure consciousness, I am Energy, I am All That Is. This sentence is also in the present tense. If we tell our subconscious mind "I want to attract a partner", we are empowering the belief that we are not ready for a partner right NOW, so our subconscious mind will not manifest a partner for us. It also empowers a belief that want equates to need. We need a partner…to be happy?

Remember by saying statements such as "I am a nice person" can also be damaging, for it can empower the belief that you have to be nice all the time. This obviously depends on what your own beliefs of being nice is. If being nice for you means always being sympathetic and paying for other peoples' bills than this can lead to you always doing that! "I am Love" is a more fitting affirmation in this context because it represents who you are and doesn't decide what you have to do, you can decide that for yourself.

Here are some affirmations. It is good to write your own affirmations for yourself, based on what you feel you are insecure about in your life – be it with relationships, career or right down to specific facets of yourself such as confidence.

"Everything is Perfect right Now. I trust the current events in my life. I know that they are leading me to my dreams."

"I radiate an ocean of warmth and happiness. People are magnetised to my unique expression."

"Today I rejoice in the miracle of life. Today I acknowledge my infinite power and let go of all my fears and insecurities. In this holy moment I surrender to the moment."

We can recite affirmations whenever we feel like it, on our way to work, on a public train, in the car. Soon it will become second nature to think positively and we will have less and less need to use affirmations as our subconscious minds are reprogrammed in Light.

Repairing through Visualisations

Visualisations are an important aspect of our way of life. This is because our subconscious mind accesses the unseen energy of the Universe, and so works through pictures and thoughts. Pictures are in essence, energetic images. Using visualisation processes, we can access the inner senses that we all possess and we can make significant changes to how we process and react to the energy of the Universe. Our spirit is so powerful that an image conjured is an image created.

By creating images within our conscious mind, our subconscious will react to these to support its sets of beliefs. For example, when we use affirmations to attract a new career, we use visualisations to energise these prayer requests. We visualise ourselves in a new career. The subconscious mind is timeless – it is beyond time. Therefore, it responds to how we are feeling in this ever-present NOW. When we visualise ourselves experiencing a new career NOW, then the subconscious mind will manifest this reality for us NOW.

Developing your own forms of visualisation are often the best. Below is an example used for cleansing the subconscious minds (**attitudinal healing**)

Imagine you are surrounded by a golden bubble – all your thoughts, feelings, emotions, desires and images are outside of this bubble.

Every time a thought, feeling or emotion arises from your subconscious mind, stop it at the gate of your bubble – and ask "is this thought loving, positive, spiritual and Divine?"

If it is then allow it into your conscious mind. If it is not then deny it entry and visualise your own Divine power transmuting negative thoughts into light. Completely checkpoint the feelings and thoughts and determine what serves you and others the best.

As we work through the next section, remember this process of spiritual growth, of enlightenment is not an easy nor a quick process – instead it is a process of awareness, the more you become aware, the more you integrate your newfound awareness into your life. The more you incorporate this wisdom, the more you transform your old modalities of limitation, fear, suffering. Whilst it may not seem quick or easy at times, it *is* infinitely rewarding as you access the limitlessness of freedom. Abundance and happiness.

Step into the arena of your soul – the playground of creation.

SECTION THREE
SOUL LOVE

This section explores the various ways in which we can give our personal power away, mostly without even realising. It examines how our fears and insecurities can distort our view of the world, leading to scarcity, limitation and pain. By understanding the reasons why we outsource our personal power, we make a fundamental step towards reclaiming that power.

Through awareness, we can draw and hold onto the infinite personal power that we all harbour. We each have the tools necessary to heal ourselves in this way. And with awareness comes the realisation of the relationship between lacking one's personal power and lacking self-love. As we begin to love ourselves more and more, we begin to access and harness the magnificent infinite power deep within.

You are not simply one being. If you choose, you can break your being up into many parts and each of those parts would be viable enough for you to greet as a friend, as a brother, as a sister. Similarly as the one being that you see yourself in the mirror, you are also a part of the Grand being that makes up all beings. As you look within, there are parts of you that require healing. There are parts of you that require love. You are many things. You are all things.

It is crucial to realise that insecurities, negative emotions are not "bad", they are simply experiences and parts of yourself. That is it. There is no polarity here apart from the one that you choose to place upon it. Insecurities are powerful signposts that you have a buried treasure of powerful strengths beneath it! In fact the most insecure people become the most confident and simultaneously sensitive through growth work. It is also a signpost that you are discovering yourself and the Universe at the same time. As you will discover, it is our insecurities that actually signpost ourselves to our destiny, revealing something far deeper and meaningful than we ever could have imagined.

It is time to remember who you are and how powerful you really are. Step out of the limitation of your own fears that imprison you in a world where you feel shy, worthless, stuck, stressed and move into a new world of confidence, power, effortlessness and joy. You are capable of anything, absolutely anything. You have all the personality traits that you desire, within you, waiting to be unleashed and harnessed. There is nothing that you cannot attain. The only blocks are your beliefs – and these are easier to dissolve than you realise.

The power that you possess is your Divine birthright. The power that you harness can create anything and it is your own to utilise. Know that you and every single other person on this planet harnesses the same power within them, so there is no need to give your power away or to take from another. You are magnificent, magical and enchanted.

Equality

Each being that exists is equal. Every single person has the same infinite powers of creation and houses the same infinite well of unconditional love.

As insecure humans, we tend to idolise others and find it necessary to place people in a hierarchical structure, including ourselves. However, the Truth is that we are each as equal as another, no matter how farther down the path others seem to be. We are each uniquely different yet infinitely similar. The world is bursting with hierarchical systems, yet these systems of status, power and control serve as an illusion to the reality of who we really are. When we look up to another as better than us we only put ourselves down.

Your greatness is just as supreme as another's. When we idolise another for their greatness we only diminish our own greatness further. There have been many great spiritual teachers and prophets that have walked the earth yet they have all taught the same message - Love yourself.

Whatever our paths, it is important to understand that each path is unique because each path is perfect for *that* Soul. Every event in your past lives and this present life has led you to this moment right NOW. It is perfection, it can be no other way for it is the embodiment of free choice/free will. There is no judgement. This isn't a test. You are not being compared to your brothers and sisters, for they have not endured the same challenges as you have, and vice versa. Instead you are bringing *your* Truth forward to expand the Whole Truth.

The Truth you hold dear to your heart is essential and crucial to the Whole. To deny that Truth is to deny the Infinite Being within and to deny the Source within is to deny the whole of existence. For you are an integral part of the whole. You are the

Divine, expressing itself in countless, varying ways. Rejoice in your expression, for you are continuously adding to the Creator's knowledge of all creation and to the knowledge of the entire Universe. Live your Truth.

Developing our personal power requires each of us to begin the path of self-discovery where we realise that we are each as Divine and Perfect as another. It is very easy to idolise another and see another as being 'better' than us. However, we find it very difficult to see the brightness within ourselves.

It is more fitting to place a mirror on your mantelpiece than to idolise an Ascended Master or spiritual leader – for it is You that you have to learn to respect and worship if you are to BE all that you are. It is you that you must endeavour to love completely if you are to realise that timeless spiritual message - You are the Oneness.

You are All That Is, You are Love. You are Infinite. You are Absolute.

Your life is a mirror

We each have a reflection. And this is not just our physical reflection in the mirror. We are each reflected by the people around us and the events that occur in our lives.

Many of us feel that we are actors on a stage with others watching and judging everything we do. While it is true that our life is symbolic of a movie being played out, it is important to realise that we are the actor, director and reviewer of this play.

Since our thoughts create our reality, everything on this plane is a mirror of our consciousness. We attract and reflect what we feel so that we can see in physical form what is happening within our consciousness. Our inner world scripts our outer reality. Therefore we are always surrounded by and are experiencing that which we are. On the physical plane, this is a way of allowing us to discover that eternal question – Who am I?

Our outer reality therefore reflects our fears, loves, insecurities and beliefs. By examining the world around us, we can better define what we are feeling within. When we are unbalanced, we usually attract those of an opposite nature to ourselves – in order to learn something from them. When we are balanced, we usually attract those who are of a similar nature. Here are some examples to better illustrate this point.

Let us take a woman who gives away her energy too much. Here, she may be trying to make everyone around her feel comfortable, born out of her own insecurities. So this woman might consistently attract men who completely take advantage of her when it comes to her relationships. Now if we look at this spiritually then we can ask why is she reflecting this in her life? What is it reflecting within? We might see that it could be a direct sign from her Infinite Self to begin to honour her own power. She has attracted and reflected what she feels inside into her outer reality – it is a message from herself *to* herself. However, if she is unaware of what she is doing she will persistently attract the same kind of man.

There are many ways in which we act out our insecurities in our relationships, however by looking deep within as to why we keep repeating the same patterns can we break these patterns and move on.

If you are surrounded by kind and loving people then this is a reflection of how you feel on the inside. If you are surrounded by people who criticise you, then this may be a reflection of you criticising yourself.

If you feel that others do not appreciate what you give them, then it is time to take a look at how open you are to receiving from others. Often many healers and those working in social care feel drained and depreciated because they are always ready to give love but find it difficult to accept and receive love.

As well as attracting and reflecting that which we are feeling on the inside, as spiritual beings, we attract or are attracted to those that we can learn from the most.

Qualities we see in our partners or friends are often qualities that we'd like to attain for ourselves. Everyone has a lesson to teach another, be it a painful one or a loving one. For example, one might constantly attract people who talk about themselves:

When you attract people who seem to be constantly talking about themselves or who seem egotistical, it may be the Universe's (through your subconscious mind) way of showing you that you aren't listening to yourself.

When we listen to that inner voice and follow our own personal truth then the Universe will respond by pushing us in the right direction. If we find ourselves becoming involved in other people's movies then we may be steered back on course through attracting what we reflect inside to show us what is actually happening. Therefore in this case we attract a lesson. How do we know what the message is? Always ask yourself, "Why is this person irritating me? What it is within me that is feeling irritation? What part of me feels uncomfortable with this other?"

The Universe is constantly sending us wonderful messages if we are willing to open our eyes and see.

Remember that the Law of Attraction works both ways. For example, if you are attracting someone who makes you feel like a victim then you have both *co-created* that reality. They, themselves have attracted you to their reality because of your feelings of inferiority and lack of self-worth. Simultaneously you have attracted them because of their ability to victimise people.

We cannot attract that which we do not already have within us. Fear attracts fear, just as Love attracts Love. The reasons may be karmic or recent, however the result is the same – for we have created the conditions for it to have manifested in the NOW (as explained in *The Law of Karma*). This mutual attraction is a learning process and if we are willing to pull ourselves out of the moment and see it for what it truly is, we can see what is on offer here. So from this example, we can use our awareness to see that the victim manifestation can be a message from our Divine Self that we have this insecurity and lack of self-worth to be resolved. We can herald these events as a prompt for us to heal and cleanse these insecurities so that we can move on and expand our consciousness and achieve greater happiness.

Also bear in mind that as well as attracting what you reflect you will often attract those to your reality that need healing – this is especially true for the more sensitive souls among you. Use your intuition to tell you if this person has been attracted to your reality because it is out of a fear on your part or if they need healing on their part. How can we tell this? Well, when we are faced with a situation we can always use our emotional base as a guide to tell us what this scenario means for us. If we feel adverse reactions to the situation, we know that we have something to learn here. If we are centred and detached and know that this person can use our help (maybe because they are experiencing something that we previously experienced in our own lives) then we approach them with compassion and offer our healing messages.

Projections

Always remember that we are constantly projecting our fears onto others, distorting the world that we see. Our internal fears are projected onto others by the Law of Reflection. Our perceptions, working through filters of fear and insecurities, see what we want to see i.e. see our fears played out or projected onto others. So in reality we understand that perception is in the mind of the beholder, where one interprets experiences and situations through their own fears - thus seeing a filtered/mosaic view of the world (our Kaleidoscope Vision). However, as the individual works through those fears, those same experiences can be viewed again and be seen completely different – they become clearer. This is the magic of awareness. The power of awareness breaks through the illusion of fears to reveal truth in its infinite form.

Projections tell us a lot about our own characters and what we are not recognising within. We are constantly projecting every moment of our existence – thus is the nature of our life on this physical plane. Our outer world is a projection of our inner world. So how are these projections different?

When we deny traits of our sSlf, we are basically denying a part of ourself that wants to be expressed. This part will not however stay denied! It will find ways of expressing itself without our knowledge – this is what is known in psychological circles as "acting subconsciously". However, our projections can cause us strife if we do not recognise them – for they will further cloud our vision of the world and further distort our kaleidoscope vision.

Let us take a simple example and look at a common situation. Let us look at Violet and Brendan who are having a coffee. Brendan is speaking to Violet and then suddenly accuses her of being moody and snappy. Violet is surprised at this sudden outburst and feels like she was simply drinking her coffee trying to listen to Brendan's story. Here, if projection is an issue then Brendan may have projected his *own* anger onto Violet and accused her of being angry. This is a projection of Brendan's inner feelings onto Violet – however it is done subconsciously without him even realising unless he becomes aware of it (or is made aware of it). This can happen in many areas of our lives or in many situations where we project our own feelings or opinions or judgements onto others without realising – this will naturally cloud our Kaleidoscope vision further and we do not see the true nature of the other individual. Instead our own issues are clouding the matter and we are essentially conversing with ourselves!

Remember, the subconscious mind is continuously manifesting, even when we sleep! So whatever is lurking within your subconscious – your insecurities, fears, opinions, judgments, will be utilised for manifestation. However, also remember this is nothing to fear or to be worried about either! It is awareness of this whole process that already initiates our release and begins the process of clearing our vision so that we better see reality.

Most projections are occurring unconsciously and seep into many conversations we have with others and the way we act and interact. The key is to find the vibration behind everything we do. Why are we saying what we are saying? What are our real motives? It is not to question everything we do but to keep our awareness high so that we are always coming from the purest place in our hearts. Which naturally serves all involves, including yourself.

Owning Your Reality

By owning everything we experience, we take ourselves away from blame, judgement and limitation as we become responsible for everything within it. What does this mean?

This means that everything we experience we understand it from our own point of view. Many people mistake this as being a narcissistic point of view, however what must be realised is that everything we each experience is passed through our kaleidoscope vision first anyway!

When we own our reality, we are understanding why experience everything the way we do. Let us take an example and look at Adam. Now Adam is getting annoyed with his friend, Debbie. Adam feels that Debbie is being way too materialistic in her lifestyle. Everything she does is money-orientated or materially focused. He finds himself getting annoyed with what she is doing and has great difficulty holding a conversation with her as he feels she is on a different wavelength, as his interests are more of a spiritual nature. So what is Adam's first reaction? His first reaction is to perceive that Debbie is doing something to annoy him and that he must react by withdrawing as he feels irritated around her.

However, already Adam has bypassed a crucial point – one that this reality is founded upon. Adam has *allowed* Debbie to annoy him. Debbie has no power over Adam's feelings. None of us have the power to make anyone feel anything! This is a crucial spiritual truth: No one has the power to make you feel anything.

Why? Because we each choose to feel the way we feel. This is the Law of Free Will. This even goes to extreme circumstances. When we are being oppressed, we feel threatened – however we only feel threatened because we have chosen to feel threatened. It is always your own choice that determines your own feelings, for it is only you that has control over your feelings!

This truth defines almost everything in spirituality – because it redefines the ultimate truth – You are a Master of *Your Own Reality*. Own Your Reality. This is the paradox – to become a master of your reality, you must first realise that you are already a master of your reality!

Returning to this example, when Adam realises this crucial point he can now look at this situation from a completely new perspective. Why is he allowing himself to become annoyed by Debbie? There is something about the way she is acting that is troubling a part of himself.

In other words, a part of himself is uncomfortable with a part of Debbie. Everything in our life is a mirror.

Each person is a reflection of who we are, who we can be, who we might be, who we could be. Every single person on this planet is a reflection of who we might have been had we lived their lives.

So this part of Debbie that is making him feel uncomfortable is a message that there is a part of himself, deep within that is insecure with the way Debbie is acting. For if it were secure, then Adam would have no problem with the way she is acting and understand through compassion that she is who she is – as is her birthright. It is when we feel agitated or animosity from those in our lives that we realise that there is something to learn here – for there is something that is stirring a part of ourselves!

When we are completely secure with who we are, then other people in our lives do not annoy us or threaten us. Another question Adam would ask himself is: Why have I created Debbie in my life?

This is a crucial point – for our life is a reflection of the way we feel inside. Our outer reality is a reflection of the inner workings of ourselves. It is a beautiful method of understanding and exploring ourselves on the physical plane. Therefore our outer world is a creation of our own devise. Every thought we have is used for manifestation on this plane through the Law of manifestation (and also through the laws of attraction and reflection)

This means that the people in our lives are there by co-creation – a means of our creating and their creating – a beautiful method of bringing together two or more people. Therefore the people in our lives are not there by accident, they are there by choice on all parts. Those that we feel animosity towards, that antagonise us – are there by conscious or subconscious creation on our part. We attract those into our lives to learn – either in a loving way or in a way that will challenge us. People can reflect a part of us – be on our wavelength- or they can be our polar opposite, to teach us something about our dark side (our shadow side) so that we may become balanced.

This is the fascinating thing about life on this planet. There is opportunity for growth everywhere we look – however this is not a school – there is a joyfulness in this growth for it is play. Children recognise that growing is something that is playful and enjoyable for it allows them to explore what they did not know before.

When we deny that those in our lives have anything to offer yet we have created them to be there – then there is a resistance for us to learn, which happens most of the time. We most often forget that the people in our lives are there by choice on both parts. We often withdraw or shrink away from those that display qualities that we do not like. But what is a quality that we do not like? What does this mean? It is a quality that we are uncomfortable with. When we are secure within, the then qualities of others will not threaten us in anyway, we will be comfortable with all.

When we own our reality, we recognise that our reality is a construct of our own making. This is nothing to fear! This is a representation of your power! You have complete control of your reality, every part of it. You can create change in any part of your reality. When you own your reality, you take back your power for it is the illusion that we do not have control over our reality that creates that illusion within ourselves that we don't have any power. Ultimately, what is occurring? We are still creating our reality – but we do it unconsciously! This is where the problems arise. For it is impossible not to create your reality, it is simply either conscious or unconscious. When it is unconscious we arise with the problems of where we are manifesting people and situations that reflect parts of ourselves that we are not dealing with. However, when we consciously face all parts of our self – then those parts that are then reflected in our outer reality will obviously be ones that are more to our liking. Meaning, when we love all parts of our self, and heal those parts of our self, those parts are reflected in our outer reality with loving people and situations. We learn to love all parts of our Self by learning to love the reflections that are represented in the people and situations around us, for they are all brought into our reality by us! When you begin to learn from those around you and recognise that no one can make you feel anything, then you realise that it is time to address why those feelings arise in you in the first place.

There is nothing that is external to you.

Nothing.

There is *nothing* that is external to you.

Acknowledging Our Present Manifestations

Instead of seeing a part of our life that we don't like in a negative light, we must first move into a space where we understand that we created that experience in reaction to an insecurity on our part. By seeing the situation as something we don't like is an immediate attack on ourselves, for we are the ones that have created that situation!

By acknowledging that your creations are a result of your thoughts and feelings of a previous time, you can subjectively and wisely see what you can learn from the situation. Then you can initiate healing to transmute the event from a painful one into a golden opportunity of growth.

You can turn *anything* you see into Light.

Let's say you are seeking a partner and find yourself constantly surrounded by couples. Everywhere you go, you can't seem to get away from them! However, the more you see this in a negative light and say to yourself, "It's so unfair, he/she is in a relationship, what about me?", the more you empower the belief within yourself that you are not worthy of such a relationship. You empower the belief that the couples are superior to yourself in some way. This then ushers your subconscious mind to manifest your fears, creating more of the same. Instead see the couples around you as a message from the Universe and your True Self that there is indeed abundance around you, so let go of your fears of scarcity and of not being loved. For, the reason you are surrounded by them is a manifestation on your part. You create your reality! And this is why we reflect our thoughts into reality, so that we may be able to see our fears in physical form in order to effectively deal with them and move on.

Accepting our present manifestations is a crucial stage in clearing our negative programming and building up our personal power. Since everything in our reality is created from our past thoughts, by acknowledging our creations, we acknowledge ourselves. We acknowledge the fact that our manifestation reflects a part of ourselves for those thoughts reflect a part of us. Therefore, we begin to understand that if we hate our manifestation, we hate a part of ourselves!

By accepting and loving the fact that we, indeed created the situation that we are presently in, we inform the subconscious mind that we do not hate that part of our-Self, instead we love that part of our-Self that reflects this manifestation. As we learn to love a troublesome manifestation in our life, and ultimately understand how and why it was created, we simultaneously heal that part of our-Self that reflected and created it! Our subconscious can only react and manifest, attract and reflect more of the same. We become more fearful, angry and separated – we miss the lesson at hand. When we resist our manifestations or anything in life, we create a blockage to the flow of love energy and we allow fear to rain on our parade. Accepting our manifestations is also a form of unconditional receiving.

By accepting our past manifestations we also empower the belief and knowledge within us that we are indeed powerful Creators. If we are constantly looking outside for someone to blame or something to blame then we are giving away our power. When we recognise the Divine, infinite power of our creative abilities by acknowledging all of our manifestations, our subconscious mind will respond by learning to believe the Truth that we are indeed Powerful Magical Creators.

In order to release yourself from the pains, sufferings and insecurities that you harbour you must be willing to analyse yourself objectively and with total honestly. Remember, no one else judges you as you do. Write down the things that you are truly insecure about, the things that you truly fear in your life. This very act of embracing your fears in such a way, embarks you on the path of self-recovery. Then combat these insecurities with affirmations to really emphasise your desire to heal and break free of them. Despite it only taking ten minutes, the Ego part of you will give many reasons not to do this! For the Ego, our traumatised GOD within, lives in constant denial and will go out of its way to hide you from your fears. However, it is when we repress and deny that we have fears that these fears breed and grow. Send love and comfort your Ego/Inner Child and embrace yourself.

There is of course a fine balance between analysing yourself objectively and being overly critical of one's own behaviour. We need to use our Angel eyes when assessing ourselves, so that we are lovingly subjective. Or we can look from the eyes of a parent as would be to a child. Here we view *ourselves* as our own child. When we shift our consciousness to that of our Infinite Self, we can look at our earthly self with that of a loving parent. We can then lovingly see where we can act or heal to gain greater happiness. We can energise our-Self with love where we need it and we can comfort ourselves with compassion in areas where we are hurting. We can see why we have acted in certain ways or why we desire the things that we do – is it because of a deeper insecurity or is it because we want happiness and joy?

Attachments

Love allows all things to be, whilst fear clings on desperately.

Love yourself. It is the epochal doctrine of spirituality. We are persistently taught to love all parts of our Self, yet most of the time we have such trouble implementing this into our lives.

On some level, we still do not fully appreciate how a lack of self-love can affect our life experience. Throughout our life, as we attempt to replenish our inner lack of self-love, we find ourselves trying to source this love externally. We attach.

Attachments are a dependency upon an externality for power/love. It is a method of replenishing what we cannot find within. We tell ourselves that external things such as money, career, substances or another person can make us happy. These attachments provide us with temporary channels to draw power (love) in order to maintain our security (happiness). Of course these sources can change and in doing so, so does our security – and ultimately our happiness. When we draw love from within, we are unaffected by external change, we are happy and secure. When we draw happiness from externalities, our happiness is reliant upon the stability of that externality – we are insecure.

As we use awareness to evaluate our experiences, we may find that we are attached in many ways and many areas of our lives.

Attachments are a defence mechanism launched to combat deep insecurities of not feeling loved. From this lack of self-love, together with a belief that we are separate, we naturally seek to source it from the outside world (externalities). We attempt to draw power/love from our friends, partners, career in order to give us security; to give us love. However, we will never be able to be secure in this way because our attachments strengthen our already existing insecurities!

When we attach ourselves to an externality we forget that we are perfect in all that we are, empowering a subconscious belief that we are *imperfect*. As we derive our happiness from this externality we stray away from our own Truth and begin to act or express in ways to accommodate it. In essence, we begin to mould ourselves to collaborate with the desires or needs of that externality in order to secure our power source. By doing this, we veer off our own personal Truth – and this causes us pain.

As we use awareness to evaluate our experiences, we may find that we are attached in many areas of our lives.

You are happiness personified – all your actions either take you away from your-Self or they bring you closer to that realisation. Let us say that you are happily walking down the street and you pass a clothes store. Inside the window is the most amazing, most glamorous and most fabulous coat you have ever seen. It's almost like this coat has been made just for you! However, you nearly trip over when you see the price tag, knowing that it is too expensive even for your impulsive nature. Now, you're unhappy because you want that coat! So you decide to save up for a few months and cost cut the non-essentials in your life. One day as you realise you have saved up enough money, you drop everything, run down to the store, grab the coat (paying for it of course) and happily walk down the street with your fantastic new coat.

However, let us take a step back. Remember that prior to your encounter with this life-changing coat, you were happy. As soon as you saw the coat and wanted it, you became unhappy as you realised you couldn't afford it. Then when you eventually bought the coat, you were happy again. So in reality, you were happy before and after your encounter with the coat. So, it was the *want* of the coat that made you unhappy. It is the want, which is synonymous with attachments, that leads to our unhappiness. For the want, like attachments, assumes that an externality can bring us happiness. As soon as our consciousness accepts this reality, we create it. We are always either consciously creating our own happiness or unhappiness. The key to transcending pain and suffering is to realise that we have all that we desire or ever need, right here, within. When we truly come to this realisation then our desires are magically fulfilled, allowing us to truly appreciate everything that comes our way.

Attachment to Others

Attachments to people are amongst the most common of problems, leading to all power games in relationships. When we attach to another, we begin to lose our sense of identity as we become more and more dependent upon seeking our power externally – through our partner, family or friends.

When we become attached to a person or a situation we immediately form a dependable relationship with that externality. In effect, we assume that we can channel power/love from that externality to make us happy.

Therefore, attachment is a dependency upon an externality for love, be it another person or an aspect of our lives, such as a money or career. When we derive our happiness from this externality, we are totally giving away our power to that aspect as we invest the security of our power within a changeable entity.

Attachments can only create a temporary state of happiness for when that situation or person changes, then we become disorientated and lose our power source.

The inside world within is unbreakable and untouchable – a reservoir of Infinite Love. The outside world is *always* changing, so why depend upon an externality for our happiness?

Let us take an example of being attached to a partner. If we derive our happiness from how this partner acts towards us then we are placing our happiness in the actions of our partner. Therefore, *our partner's state of being determines our individual happiness*. Ultimately, we have given away our power to our partner.

We are making a powerful statement here! We are saying, "You control my happiness. Here have my power!" When our partner is angry, we become upset because they are not sending us Love. *They* control our state of being. When they are happy with us, we draw on their power for this Love and become more and more dependent on them for our own happiness. This line of thought also empowers the belief within our subconscious mind that we are not worthy of determining our own happiness. We inform our subconscious that we need love from this other person in order to be happy – therefore manifesting an outer reality where we become weaker and more needy. As we all know, people change their moods from moment to moment, this is the nature of being. So why place your happiness in such instability?

Know that internally you are permanently connected to Source. Therefore you have everything you need. When you realise and understand this Truth, *nothing* can harm you.

Many conditions are a result of attachment. Peer and societal pressure is one example of attachment. It is an attachment to how others think of you. It is a dependency upon other peoples' opinions determining your own happiness. This is a result of conditioning where we have been taught to value the opinions of others over our own. It is time to abandon this limiting philosophy! Realise that you control your own happiness, you always have! You either give that control to another or you retain it for yourself. However, remember even when you give your control to another you are still controlling your happiness by continuously giving that control away!

When we truly love another, then we allow that other to express themselves in their own unique way. Similarly, they allow *us* to express ourselves in our own special way. There is no attachment to how each should or should not act. This is because we are loving *ourselves* first! When you source the love from within yourself, there is no need to attach, for you are empowered with love and light. You are loved…by You! Remember you are constantly creating from this very present moment. As we derive our happiness from an externality we stray away from our own Truth and begin to act or express in ways to accommodate it. In essence, we begin to mould ourselves to collaborate with the desires or needs of that externality in order to secure our power source. By doing this, we veer off our own personal Truth – and this also causes us pain.

Know that You are Perfect right NOW. You have everything you seek within. It has always been there and will always be there. You have a direct link to the infinite Source of all love and all wisdom. There is no need to attach to an externality for power, for the reservoir within you is home to Divine Power and Love. Drawing on your own power leaves you free to be, express and manifest. It also empowers potent messages to your subconscious informing it that you *are* powerful yourself – boosting your confidence and positively affecting every decision, thought, feeling and action you make in your life.

ATTACHMENT TO CONCEPTS

The world is rich with potential attachments. Whilst people are the most obvious, we also harbour many attachments in our lives related to concepts such as money, career, food and stimulants. Whilst these may seem completely unrelated, it is our relationship to everything in our lives that defines our relationship to Self. For example, a man who feels dependent upon alcohol has developed an attachment to this substance in order to derive power/love from it. He tells himself that by drinking, he will feel better and life will be easier - in effect he has created the illusion that alcohol can provide him with the power/love that each and every one of us so desperately desires. However, we already know the consequences of this. By depending upon this attachment, this alcohol, this man effectively gives his own power away - internalising the belief that he needs this substance in order to be happy. His internal framework will create the belief that he is then weak and needy and delude this individual into believing he is fully dependent upon it. However, it is a societal illusion that we need anything external to derive our happiness from! If this man gathers his courage then he may realise that this dependency is doing him more harm than good as he outsources his power to this attachment. Through perseverance this man may break free of his attachment, his dependency, and his outcome becomes pure spiritual growth. Not only has he returned to the realisation that power/love is from within, dramatically empowering the Self, but he has taken the golden wisdom gained from his attachment experience - propelling him to even further happiness than he had prior to his drinking. Of course, we do not need to suffer in order to grow! It is through awareness of our suffering that brings us growth. However, once we reach this awareness we are aware that we do not need to suffer in order to grow! Thus we grow from immediate awareness of our experiences and forgo suffering.

Food is very similar. We can form attachments with food to derive love (happiness) or as a method of protecting ourselves from attack, which itself is a form of drawing power from it. In reality, food has no power! It is only us that gives it power. You are a grand being with extraordinary power that whatever you direct your attention to with intention will burst with power.

Money, career also affect us in the same manner. If we are depending upon our career to derive all our happiness from life then in essence we are distracting ourselves with this concept. Of course our careers should make us happy and bring us happiness! However, if we are pursuing a notion in our minds that we must have a certain career to maintain a certain amount of security then this is a complete reflection of how we feel about ourselves. We are assuming that we need our career, an external attachment, in order to maintain internal security, our happiness. This will only make us more insecure! Similarly, if we are drawing our happiness from a desire to attain a certain amount of money then our happiness will be determined by that experience. However, we will never be truly happy because as soon as we attain that money, we will set ourselves a new goal that will bring us happiness – we will continually seek happiness for we continue to believe it to be external!

A rich man's happiness, based on his wealth, will fluctuate according to his outside world – his job, his car, his house. And so, he will desperately try to control everything outside himself to secure his happiness. However, if these externalities are challenged then this man immediately becomes very unhappy. The truth is that everything we need is within. If the rich man is truly secure in his own happiness within, then he will be happy before his wealth materialised and after it has disappeared – leaving him free *always*. Once we are content with being ourselves and expressing ourselves we do not need to source our power from another. We can never be harmed externally either despite the many changes that occur.

ATTACHMENT TO TIME

Our pre-occupation with Time is one of our biggest battles to overcome.

The concept of Time is fascinating because it is malleable to fit our individual perceptions. The theory of simultaneous time – where the past, present and future occur concurrently – is not new. Throughout the ages of man, both science and spirituality have entertained this concept. Einstein is renowned for saying, "People like us, who believe in physics, know that the distinction between past, present, and future is only a stubbornly persistent illusion." While our logical mind has real trouble grasping this notion, it is superfluous for us to fully understand the schematics of how it works, just *why* it works.

It is only our perception that creates what we see. When we look into the past, we can see it in either Love or in fear. Two people can walk away from the same event but have two completely different versions of history. These past events can then change *further* according to the observer's ever changing present state of mind. Look back at an event in your life that you have always thought of as painful – this event has defined your present view of the world and ultimately moulds your future. From this place of pain, you theorise how you should act in similar situations, shaping your world.

Children are the eternal teachers when it comes to learning about forgoing our attachment to time. Children do not feel the need to attach to the past or the future, they simply exist in the timeless present moment. They are free to express and free to grow at incredible rates because of this ability to surrender to the moment.

LETTING GO OF THE PAST

The past is a wonderful concept because it allows us to assess our manifestations from the present. We can examine what has led to our present manifestations by looking at our past thoughts and behaviour. In effect, we are able to access a psychological profile of ourselves.

However, the past can also hold us back in many ways. It can act like quicksand, pulling us down and back, eventually consuming us. This is because we tend to allow past events to dictate our present and future actions. It is through the fear of what happened once will happen again. This only attracts more of the same!

The key to escaping quicksand is to stop fighting it! We are free when we relax, let go and wait for the release. The Past has something to teach us and if we are willing to learn we can live fuller lives in the eternal present moment.

When we allow one event to affect the rest of our present and future decisions, we become trapped by our own limited view of the world. The key to the past's significance lies in its opportunity for growth. We often play out scenarios over in our minds to find who has been wronged. The Ego (fearful part of us) naturally cannot understand that there can be two winners from a situation, because the Ego does not understand that infinite power can be drawn from within ourselves. The Ego's base belief of everything being finite naturally makes it believe there is scarcity in the world. This then leads to us theorising that we need to outsource power to externalities based on this scarcity.

By remaining in the past we can continually get pulled into power battles where our traumatised Ego searches through past events and replays them over and over until either:

- We are continually seen as the victim (victim syndrome), or
- We become powerful and seem the temporary victor (victor syndrome)

VICTIM SYNDROME

Whenever we feel sorry for ourselves by thinking back on a past event where we have been hurt, we create the illusion to ourselves that we are in fact a victim. This belief is passed onto the subconscious mind, which in turn manifests it into our physical reality. Therefore this will lead to more future manifestations where we are in fact a victim again.

Let us look at a woman who has been very hurt by a loved one in the past and feels betrayed. Here, she may constantly loop this betrayal in her mind. This will no doubt seriously detriment her present freedom and reshape her world into a fearful place, where she is a victim. However, once she challenges her Ego (her hurt inner child) to see exactly what's happening, she may realise that no one was to blame. She may see that at that time, she may have attracted the situation born out of insecurities about being betrayed or that she simply experienced it to bolster her confidence in new ways that others would not experience themselves. Whatever the reason, there is no blame for having created it, it is more of a celebration that this insecurity has finally been exposed for healing so that it will never manifest again. By facing your fears you ensure that they do not reappear – you have transmuted them into the wisdom of Light.

Most of our insecurities are born out of our childhood and adolescence. For example, there are those who keep others at a distance as a self-defence mechanism born out of an earlier rejection, maybe by their own parents. So some people will ensure that others are at a distance or end relationships first so that they cannot be rejected themselves. We can, however, break all things down into the present moment and heal things from here. When we do this, the past will simultaneously be healed. Many may stipulate that the blame lies with the parents in this particular case. However, blame serves no one and definitely does not serve the child, for it only creates the belief that this child is more of a victim.

The key to breaking free of these repetitive patterns is to understand the lesson, forgive and transcend. Remember forgiveness is not saying that the other was right, it is saying that you are no longer willing to carry the burden of pain. It says that whatever happened in childhood or in the past has given you the strength and wisdom that you possess right NOW. We all know that suffering leads to greater awareness. However, we need to understand when to stop suffering when we have this awareness! When we look at where we are NOW we see that indeed certain sufferings have led us to be stronger in our efforts to resist them. The child in this case now sees themselves as less of a victim and does not hold the belief that they have been wronged. When you break free from these patterns of blame, guilt and bitterness a whole new world awaits you – one where nothing can hold you back, you are born anew in each moment. There is meaning behind *everything*.

The victim syndrome includes situations where we see *ourselves* as having done something 'wrong' as well. When you perceive yourself as having acted 'wrong' in the past, this only attracts more of the same as it empowers the belief that you *are* wrong. Instead, see yourself as having acted as the best you knew how in that holy instant. And this is not a pretence, it is a Truth. Everything is perfection and each act is born of pure free will on your behalf. The events in your life, the emotions you felt, the pains you suffered all lead to you make each and every decision that you make in life. It is Perfection, for you were acting as you *only* knew how at that time. Anyone living your life will act exactly the same if they experienced the same experiences you experienced! The key to prevent a similar situation from repeating is to see your past events as total Perfection; and then using Awareness to evolve. Remember, you are expanding universal consciousness through your explorations.

You do not have to apologise for your perceived mistakes. Instead take responsibility for what you have done and realise the consequences and repercussions, not from the eyes of blame but that of an enlightened person. See with your Angel Eyes. Be willing to look at that part of you that created that perceived mistake in the Light of Love.

When we label a part of us as wrong and distance ourselves from it then that part of us is energised even more. Accept things for having happened the way they did and congratulate yourself for having yet another facet of yourself opened to the wisdom of your magnificent Light. It is only when we separate ourselves from fear (and from *anything* for that matter) that it causes us pain.

When we look back at a past event and find that we are angry towards another, what our traumatised Ego wants the other to say is "Yes, I'm sorry I hurt you. You were right and I was wrong." By hearing this, the Ego is at peace because it feels that it has won the situation and drawn power/love from the other (the loser).

However, this is temporary for our fears are still present and will manifest again. If we look deeper, we see the spiritual underlying message of our reasons for being angry. What we want is for that person to love us and vice versa. By wanting that other person to say 'I was wrong' is really a call out to say 'yes I was wrong and I do love you'. The Ego always stops short of fully understanding the meaning behind everything we do. This is why we must endeavour to use the philosophies of our Infinite Self rather than that of our traumatised Ego (the fear-based part of our-Self).

Pain in another person is their own pain but they may project it onto others because they want love and attention. For example, take a person who lives his life through intimidating others. This may be born out of a deep insecurity developed as a child, let's say from a tyrannical parent. So, whenever this individual encounters people he intimidates them, seeking power from them to make himself feel better about his deep fears of not being loved. He has become a slave to his fears and insecurities – where his Ego believes that no one loves him and that people might intimidate him like his parent. In this respect he feels he has to act first and gain power in this way as well. What he is really doing of course is calling out for Love! However, he has allowed his past events to dictate his own actions in his present world. His past pain has shaped his present world because he is listening to the philosophies of his fears (through his Ego). Ultimately, his present world is a fearful place where you must attack first before others attack you.

Often we will replay events and draw power from those who have hurt us – or fantasise about possible future scenarios where we are more powerful than these people. These 'plays' are just veils from the real truth that we need to acknowledge. Firstly, we are attached, outsourcing our power – dependent upon this externality – other people. And this is that these people, if they have hurt us, have simply brought out pain that was already existent within us. Remember, pain reflects ignorance – parts of us that have yet to be blessed with wisdom. We are wiser after our suffering not before. Yes, we may have been happy before our pain but we still harboured parts of our-Self that had not been accessed or dealt with. After our suffering and after our healing of that suffering, we become wiser. Ultimately, this new wisdom leads to an even greater happiness than we experienced before.

So our painful experiences reflect our insecurities and should we choose, we can move beyond these fears and emerge stronger and victorious. We cannot be hurt by someone or something if there isn't already an insecurity within us that is open to be hurt in this manner. This is why, with all the strengths and weaknesses that we harbour, the parts of our-Self that we feel confident about do not get offended by others. It is only the weaknesses that are vulnerable to attack. When you are truly secure in your-Self, then nothing can harm you.

DETACHMENT: HOW TO RELEASE THE PAST

Learning to detach ourselves first involves learning to *respond* to situations rather than reacting to them. This means learning to respond to emotionally charged situations in the past (and present for that matter) rather than attaching ourselves to them and allowing them to consume us. Emotions are the fuel of attachments – because emotions are the fuel of everything we do! Once we learn to embrace and release an emotion then we are free to move forward and not stagnate.

If we are faced with a powerful emotional situation and find ourselves constantly playing scenarios in our mind of how things could, should, would have worked – then we are focusing all of our energy into the past or the future and ignoring the crucial present moment, where all manifestations are born. One way of pulling yourself out of emotionally attached past events is to literally pull your consciousness out of the situation. This is the art of detachment.

Stop for a moment and realise who you are – who you *really* are. You are a Spiritual Being having a human experience. Lift yourself higher and higher and see that you are merely submerged in a movie that you wrote, directed and are playing out. It is a movie. You are and have always been in total control. During the times where you believe you had no power, you simply deluded yourself into this illusion – this is your power! What you have become so attached to is a result of your emotional and Ego-desire body – realise that these are merely illusions in themselves. The only constant, the only reality is *You* – consciousness, Love, existence.

You can now look at others in your life that may be contributing to this feeling of intense attachment and realise that they, too, are a Soul playing in a movie. As we look around we see that we are all brothers and sisters playing in our movies. We see that we become attached to one or another because it is part of the movie we have scripted with one another through our manifestations, attractions and reflections. Yet we can similarly pull ourselves out through awareness. This is not to dismiss the movie that is our life, since what we experience is important to us. It is also not to say that we deserved anything in our lives. Instead it is a message that everything has purpose of growth.

It is through awareness where we find our freedom and are able to see the situation for what it truly is. It is here where we can assess what the lessons are to be learned from this experience and it is from this vantage point, high up in the clouds that we can see that we have simply got caught up in the process. You will feel a wonderful sense of release and relief in this moment of freedom and realise that attachments can be so blinding if we allow our emotions to consume us. It is very easy to be consumed by emotions and past events, so don't be hard on yourselves. Congratulate yourselves on being aware NOW and having been brave to experience such powerful, explosive situations.

If you see yourself as having made a lot of mistakes in the past, then you will continue to manifest mistakes in your present and the future. This is because you are empowering the belief within yourself that you make mistakes! Understand that *there are no mistakes*, just moments of free will – because free will heralds exploration and learning. Perceived mistakes are actually golden opportunities for spiritual growth – see them in the light of your wisdom. See perceived mistakes as challenges which you have successfully overcome or as challenges that lie wait to *be* overcome. Seeing them in this light will empower the belief that you are strong and do not need suffering to grow. Surrounding your perceived mistakes in love and by loving that part of yourself for showing you the pain within you, empowers the belief that you do indeed love yourself. This, therefore attracts others who love yourself in equal measure.

Learn to laugh at yourself when you feel embarrassed or annoyed at something you've done. When we laugh at a part of our-Self, we are undergoing an important psychological step. We are challenging that insecurity within us to come forth behind its shield. We let go of our incessant need for everything to be perfect and acknowledge that even things we perceive as wrong or embarrassing are in reality perfection. Don't you find that those who can laugh at themselves, you feel much more at ease around?

They radiate confidence when they see the laughter in everything. They are simply free to express. So are you!

Writing is also another brilliant way of releasing and centring our being from all the attachments and distractions of our daily lives. Write down your feelings and thought processes if you feel stuck in a past event. This allows you to effectively see your attachments. The very process of writing down your feelings allows you the space to then detach from them, for you are releasing those feelings through your writing. This also allows you to see how these past events are affecting you NOW. Writing allows us to directly see that which we are often so oblivious to acknowledging. As we effectively force our thoughts onto paper, it cannot persist to jumble around like it would in our minds. Instead, we are able to take a look at our thoughts from a subjective point of view and begin to see correlating patterns and distinct conditionings and attachments.

Of course, meditation and being still provides us with such comfort and wisdom – because it is here where we are constantly reminded that we are susceptible to the whims of the emotional body and attachments to externalities. By bringing a state of stillness into our lives, we train ourselves with the understanding that life is much more enjoyable through the art of detachment.

LETTING GO OF THE FUTURE

Just as we are attached to the past, we are similarly attached to the future!

When you are truly happy with yourself and are ambivalent about future occurrences, then the world truly becomes your playground as you embrace limitless possibilities. This is because when you expect, you are blocking the flow of energy.

Expectations by definition create limitations on your manifestations and the Universe's manifestations for you. When we attach ourselves to an idea, we put all our energy into that idea and become so attached that we expect a specific outcome. Having expectations limits our manifestations since we form a kind of tunnel vision and block out what else the Universe might be trying to show us. Focusing on one outcome will then cause us bitter disappointment if it doesn't occur.

By accepting all, you are making a profound statement – you allow energy to flow freely and thus allow the limitless wonders of abundance to drift within your grasp. When we look into the future, we lose sight of the present moment – and this is where all manifestations are born.

We often say to ourselves 'I will be happy when I have more money, when I lose more weight, when I have that job.' These are all attachments and they all speak a clear message "I am not happy with who I am *now*!" Even when you get that job, have more money or lose more weight, you will still be searching for that happiness because you still believe it to be external.

When you live in the future, you are longing to be something else – sending a clear message to your subconscious that you are not happy with who you are at this present moment. The subconscious reacts to everything we feel and think by influencing our present decisions, thoughts and feeling. Be aware of what you are empowering within yourself.

Always endeavour to remember that You are Perfect NOW. You have always been Perfect and will always be Perfect. You are that eternal spark of GOD, nothing can change that. It is only our doubts over our own Divinity that can put a veil over this eternal Truth. Break away those judgments of your-Self and move closer to that timeless fact. As we see the brilliance within ourselves then and only then will others reciprocate and see our magnificence too.

Trust that the Universe has plenty to offer you. Do not feel that you must know what your future is so that you can feel secure. Trust that not knowing is better than knowing. Remember, unknowingness is the playground of the Soul – it is here where miracles dwell. Die to the past as you embrace the present. Die to the future as you embrace the present further. Totally surrender yourself to the eternal NOW. Cleanse your mind of expectations so that you may fully enjoy the wonders of existence. When you love yourself for who you are, you are sending a powerful message to your subconscious, you are telling it that you are happy NOW – your subconscious will instinctively react by creating happy, loving manifestations NOW.

Remember we are constantly creating from this very present moment. Children are perpetual teachers when it comes to learning about forgoing our attachment to time. Children do not feel the need to attach to the past or the future, they simply exist in the eternal present moment. They are free to express and grow at incredible rates because of this ability to surrender to the moment.

Remember it is your relationship to everything in your life that defines your relationship to Self. It is also your relationship to Self that defines your relationship to everything else. Your life is a mirror of your consciousness. Also remember that if you recognise attachments in your life, it is not something to view negatively – instead it is a potential source of immense spiritual growth! Through detachment, you transmute insecurities within you into powerful aspects of wisdom. There is purpose to everything in your life.

As we let go of the attachments in our lives, we express a powerful statement. We send a clear message to the Spirit within that we realise and acknowledge our power. As we detach, we surrender the illusions that claim externalities have power. Remember power is synonymous with love. As you source power from within to ensure your security, you are loving yourself. This is the most powerful form of existence. When you love yourself, you are the epitome of understanding, compassion and awareness. You are in the position to truly love and appreciate others and to truly love and appreciate the life that you lead.

Let go of the shackles of attachments. Surrender to yourself. Recognise the ultimate freedom that enters your consciousness when you state "I am". There is nothing greater than who you are. True freedom is the arena of the Soul – the grand playground of possibility.

Deep within is an infinite reservoir of Love. Deep inside is a source of infinite wisdom, infinite resources and infinite power. Journey within to meet the most sacred, powerful and divine being – the Source of all that is…You.

Embracing Your Dark Side

In spirituality, it is very easy to focus on the light and positive aspects of Self, yet deny the dark and negative attributes we all possess. Just as the night follows day to collectively make the whole, we are both the light and the dark. You are All That Is.

The nature of this plane, of duality, is to segregate the day into day and the night into night, so we see aspects of ourselves and others as good or bad, positive or negative.

In essence, our mission is to overcome duality through the power of Compassion – the embodiment of unconditional love. Compassion is the highest frequency in the Universe because it has the ability to see the power and purpose of all things – the Light *and* the Dark.

Compassion therefore allows us to view the Dark in a completely different manner. Here we see that the Dark is not simply 'bad', but a place that requires love, healing and attention. The Dark is a place where Light has yet to reach – *it is an absence of Light!* As we endeavour to heal our darkness we are offered explosive opportunities for growth, leading to greater happiness. Therefore *negative traits are really positive ones in disguise!* They are strengths disguised as weaknesses. It is how we use these attributes that define our ability to totally unconditionally love. If we deny negative traits within us, then we are further segregating ourselves from other parts of our-Self!

The darkness within represents the unknown, that which we have not yet explored. Therefore, the Dark represents the ignorance within. It is through wisdom that we bring Light into these areas. By turning your attention to a part of yourself that needs healing, you are focusing your Light on that Dark aspect. What happens when you shine a light in the darkness? The darkness is immediately transmuted into light. Ignorance becomes wisdom.

As we deal with the various facets of our-Self and move to a more enlightened state of being, we will naturally bring Light to all parts of our-Self. This is the quintessence of en-Light-enment – to empower with Light.

Using compassion, we can turn any Dark aspect that we encounter into a higher frequency.

Embracing our dark side first requires us not to fear the dark within ourselves. It is when we fear a part of our-Self that we project it onto another. One way of spotting whether we are denying a part within us is through our judgements. When we point a finger at another being and claim that we could never relate to them because they are 'evil' or 'power-hungry' or 'egotistical', then in essence we deny a part of ourselves. We all have access to all the negativity that has ever been played out in the history of this planet. This is because we are all the same at our very core – All That Is. However, what defines each and every being is how we approach these traits within us. Do we deny these traits, thereby allowing them to fester and grow, or do we see the importance of these virtues in teaching valuable lessons about ourselves, thereby allowing *us* to grow.

Strong emotions such as anger, blame and guilt can do us much more harm if we deny that they exist within us and focus on trying to be nice all the time. We have to be honest with ourselves if we really desire to be free of such negative states of being. Remember that our subconscious mind always knows our true state of being, so it is really pointless to lie or deny an insecurity within us! It will only be manifested in greater form to give us a bigger spiritual kick up the backside.

When we feel a negative emotion, it is important that we do not attempt to ignore it. This may seem like a paradox as we are persistently told not to dwell on the negative, indeed, spirituality teaches us to maintain positive thoughts in order to have this reflected in our outer reality and to learn self-love. However, remember that as we endeavour to be positive, it is our responsibility to deal with the negative parts (our insecurities) that we already possess.

Let us take an example and look at a woman who strives to live her life positively. Every day Gemma endeavours to maintain positive thoughts and to be nice to those around her. Now let us assume that Gemma is having a lot of trouble with her partner, who belittles her about everything she does. Gemma does not want to be negative or cause tension and so ignores the anger that is swelling at the way she is being treated.

This is a very common situation, where in an effort to be positive we ignore the negative. Without even realising, by approaching life in this manner we have polarised to the other extreme – to the Light!

In this case, Gemma is forgoing her own happiness in an effort to be 'nice'. She believes she is being positive by ignoring her anger but in reality she is *suppressing* her anger. This suppressed anger will then turn foul and affect other areas of her life. When we ignore a negative attribute that emerges, we are ignoring the dark within us that requires love (light). We are distancing ourselves from another part of our-Self. If you had three children, would you choose to love only two because they were good and behaved properly? Of course not! You would love all unconditionally. Learning to unconditionally love our-Self means learning to love *all* parts of our-Self, without conditions!

By applying the power of compassion to all areas of our life we see that there is purpose to both the Light and the Dark. In this case, Gemma may see that her anger is a message from her soul saying, "Hey! Heal this part of me!" Compassion allows her to see purpose in her Dark aspect as she uses awareness to evaluate what her pain is trying to tell her. Maybe it is teaching her to be more resilient or to stand up for herself. Ultimately, the feeling or thought reveals there is a part within that is in pain and requires love and attention. Using awareness, the Dark is transformed into Light; ignorance is transformed into wisdom.

We know that negative traits in the form of insecurities have powerful ways of raising our awareness when they surface. For example, a man who has a quick temper may alienate those around him because of this trait. This man can allow this trait to rule him, leading him to all kinds of assumptions about the world and himself, energising the already strong emotions he often feels. Alternatively, this man can look within and see the trait as something to be healed. He can transmute the trait into something far more magical and powerful by acknowledging that he has indeed got a quick temper. The energy used for his anger can be channelled into a positive trait such as passion. Ultimately, it is the realisation that by looking within and healing himself that this man has raised his awareness – therefore increasing his happiness.

By healing and dealing with our own dark traits, can we better understand ourselves and therefore others. We begin to look less at others with judgement and more with compassion. We move into a space where we understand the nature of peoples' behaviour and therefore are able to help them understand their own behaviour from a place of Love.

The more we face our fears and insecurities, the sooner we can heal and deal with them and move on. We all desire happiness – a harmony of our emotions where we can feel positive and vibrant at all times. And this is achieved not by focusing purely on the Light already within us but by *bringing* Light into all parts of our-Self.

Love *all* parts of your-Self.

ACKNOWLEDGING YOUR DARK SIDE

Emotions are there to be felt *and* released. Emotions are essentially energy-in-motion. To stop this movement by repressing or ignoring is to deny a natural state of being! Releasing negative emotions such as anger, blame, shame and guilt is simply releasing energy stored within. We can either let it remain within, eating away at the rest of our being or we can channel it out and see it for what it really is. Psychologically, as we release, our subconscious mind is reconditioned and will reflect this in our manifestations as well as our thoughts, feelings, actions and decisions in life.

You have always had the ability to be your own therapist. In this respect, as you encounter a negative emotion or thought, you can undertake a two-part thought process.

- First, ask yourself why the emotion has emerged.
- Secondly, ask if *someone else* is involved in your emotional turbulence.

Embracing and releasing emotions are crucial processes both spiritually and psychologically. As you embrace and release you become aware of how that emotion has taken a hold of you and then begin the process of understanding *why* it has taken a hold of you.

Let us take an example and look at a pair of friends – Rich and Annabel. Now, Annabel is angry with Rich for being over-invasive with his energy. Annabel feels that Rich unloads his problems but does not seem to have time to listen to *her* problems! And so Annabel becomes increasingly upset at being taken advantage of. However, Annabel feels that to say something would be confrontational and 'negative'.

There are two lessons here. Firstly, it is spiritually conducive for Annabel's growth to look within herself for the reasons she is feeling this way and not blame another for it; only something unhealed within us is open to attack. Pain can only be felt if it is within us to begin with. A truly en-Light-ened being, of pure unconditional love, would not be harmed by anything externally for there is nothing within them open to harm!

So in this example, Annabel would first ask – Why is this situation affecting her? Using the Laws of Reflection and Attraction, Annabel would ask if the situation is a lesson from the Universe telling her to listen to *herself* more? Is Annabel distracting herself from her own life by listening to others' problems and thereby ignoring her own life? It is all very well helping others but if we feel adversely then we know, we sense, that something isn't right.

The second lesson is for Annabel to honour her own power and express herself, compassionately.

So as well as looking within, it is important for Annabel to inform Rich of how she feels, for Annabel cannot deny that she is feeling *something*. She must endeavour to acknowledge her emotion whatever it may be. Simultaneously, Rich may himself have something to learn from this – maybe to begin to listen more to others through their discussion?

By controlling ourselves to not express anything 'bad' will only energise that emotion or thought further! A negative (dark) emotion or thought is only 'bad' because we deem it to be so. This is more duality consciousness! Using Compassion, we see the purpose in *everything*. We use our awareness and love to heal our Darkness, rewarding ourselves with a new learned strength.

The purpose, of course, is to release the emotion or thought before it becomes anger! Anger is an energy that establishes blame, either with the perpetrator or the recipient. It can also be formed through resentment where we have not been honest with our feelings in the first place and then over time harbour feelings of anger towards another. We are in effect asking for this other person to be psychic and read our minds!

In essence, our anger is a belief that we is being victimised. The subconscious mind can only read this as – "People victimise me. This means others have power over me. Therefore I am powerless!" This will negatively affect every thought, feeling and action in our lives. The more we practice to embrace and *express* what we feel, the more skilled we become at highlighting and rapidly healing the dark within us. Subsequently, we become more confident, secure and happy.

By ignoring your dark emotions, you pretend that it's not there. By focusing purely on the Light or positive parts of yourself, you turn your attention away from your dark aspect and do not send it love, which it desperately wants!

The more we practice to embrace what we feel and to express it, the more and more aware we become of ourselves. This means that we become better and better skilled in highlighting so-called dark emotions within us, those that require healing, before we project it onto others.

If we endeavour to use compassion, we can honour both our-Self and the other. Let us take another example where anger has already been formed. Let us take a look at a relationship where one partner expresses their anger towards their beloved over the amount of time they spend at home. Obviously, we know the problems that can ensue if this emotion is kept within, it will grow and emerge as an explosion in one big fight later on! However, let us assume that the partner has taken the courage to express their true feelings. This anger expressed, releases those thoughts and feelings that have not had the opportunity of the wisdom of Light. These thoughts and feelings have been harbouring within this partner for some time (to lead to this negative emotion). The other partner, who has been spending less and less time at home, will have been subconsciously picking up on these emotions but not consciously aware, so new manifestations would have already been forming. The expression of the emotion, however, allows the situation 'to come to Light.' This is very important. It allows us to see the other person's point of view but more importantly brings our feelings to the surface so that we may finally deal with them ourselves. It is our own awareness of our own feelings that helps us to grow.

DIALOGUING WITH YOUR DARK SIDE

We often feel like we hear a voice in our heads that chastise us, that punish us continually for having said or done something 'wrong'. This voice, if we allow it, can grow to become the most dominant voice in our heads, in which case it will cause us tremendous stress and discomfort.

The first thing to recognise is that this voice is a part of you – it is literally crying out for help! Our initial response however is to listen to it, primarily because on some level we agree with this voice and harbour feelings of unworthiness. Recognising that this voice is a part of us will help us from suppressing this voice and subsequently our resulting feelings of anger and self-hatred.

The next step is to dialogue with the voice, speak to the voice. This is not done by confronting this voice each time it tells us off or completely ignoring it. Instead it requires questioning the voice and probing it to ask why?

Let us take an example and say that you have just seen an advert for a job you would love to pursue. You're initially excited and then out of the blue - a voice enters your head, totally uninvited:

"You can't do that job, you're not good enough." ; What about the job you're in now? It's secure" ; "Do you know how many other people are going to apply for that same job? What are the chances that *you* would get it?".

The voice predominately repeats this saying over and over again. Our first instinct is to listen to this and feel worthless.

However, if we begin to dialogue with this voice we recognise why it thinks the way it does. We can ask the voice to explain itself, to carry on in its statement. "You can't do that job because…because you're not good enough" , "because probability says you won't get it" , "because others are better than you". The more we speak to this voice the deeper we get towards where this voice is emenating from – a fear, an insecurity relating to our self worth. Fear of failure or a feeling of worthlessness or fear of not being good enough. The voice is afraid and so projects fearful theories about the world. This voice is a part of you. It is a scared part of you that only knows fear because it this is what it knows best. This voice is the Ego, the hurt Inner Child. Or can be seen as an aspect of you, for you can see yourself as many parts, many sub-personalities. The key is to recognise that this voice is hurt and the remedy for pain and fear is love and wisdom.

When you turn your attention towards this part of you and 'shine your Light' upon it, you begin the powerful process of transformation. That voice will at first attempt to challenge the light, loving thoughts that are now countering its philosophy on life. However, by understanding where the voice comes from, you heighten your awareness to realise that this voice is ignorant as it does not know any better. You realise that this voice only knows what it knows because of the fearful experiences and conditionings it has learnt from the outside – through you! As you change you, you change *you*.

Direct your love towards it, towards yourself. Begin to recognise any feeling that is self-critical as a part of you that has never grown up from childhood or adolescence. Notice in your life whenever you feel that you are punishing yourself. If you feel you said something 'wrong', acted in a way that you regretted, comparing yourself with others, feel that you are incapable of doing something – if you hear a voice that is chastising you – recognise it! This voice is a reflection of your insecurities. It is a cry out for help. Challenge the voice and bring about your own logic – that of your Infinite Self – the logic of a higher being. Bring in the wisdom of Love and recognise that you capable of *every*thing, you cannot do *any*thing wrong, you are perfectly special and unique.

Soften the voice with love and kindness, be gentle as you would with a child. Inform the voice that it does not need to fear, it does not need to believe it is unworthy. You are in effect speaking to your inner child. Or psychologically, you are using your conscious mind to retrain your subconscious.

METHODS IN RELEASING EMOTIONS

There are many methods of channelling and dealing with our dark side – that which needs healing. Remember, simply releasing at others is not the solution! We must endeavour to recognise and express that which we feel in order that it does not turn into anger, resentment, blame etc… Of course, we find that we already have stored dark emotions that do require releasing. The first is to recognise that within we have stored energy-in-motion that has been suppressed or ignored. When you have a block in your drain what do you do? You unblock the drain! It is important following awareness to acknowledge that there is this energy that's wants out.

Meditation is a very popular method of dealing with adverse emotions. Here the emotion is looked upon through the eyes of subjectivity – through the compassionate eyes of our Infinite Self. By looking at yourself from a neutral point of view through detachment you can assess why you feel this negative emotion and see the inherent value from this event/emotion/situation.

Of course, for some it can be difficult to remain neutral whilst fully experiencing such an emotion. So another very effective method is writing. When we write our angry or upset words, we become fully aware of what we are actually feeling. This is a powerful form of release. Too often, the emotions and thoughts that roam around in our heads are cluttered, chaotic and formless. This allows our traumatised Ego to take over and assume control, trying to find out who is the winner and who is the loser of this play inside our minds. That is your fears speaking, for we know there are no losers in reality, only winners. So, when we write out these words of how we feel and what is actually making us angry, we are instantaneously performing a cleansing ritual. On an energetic level we are releasing and transmuting masses of dense vibrational energies – 'negative' emotions. On a mental level we are allowing the emotion to show itself directly to us instead of hiding behind the Ego, so that we can deal with it using our reasoning. On a spiritual level, we are able to take the wisdom from the situation and move on using Compassion.

Another way to release anger is exercise – this is an excellent method of releasing stored negativity. By stimulating the physical body, we speed up the energy flow within and force negativity (a heavy vibration) out of our naturally loving states of being. Some people prefer this method. Punching a pillow or sprinting furiously can be other effective ways of releasing negativity - notice how good you feel afterwards? Whatever we do, it is important that we acknowledge where and why the emotion surfaced.

CRYING

Crying is often labelled as a time of weakness, a time where one breaks down. However, let us look at this concept from that of a compassionate being. Crying is a surrender of control, a willingness to totally embrace a felt emotion. Usually, we endeavour to control all of our negative emotions by inhibiting them, only allowing them to fester and grow and turn foul. Crying is in fact a powerful form of release, where we are saying "I surrender. I release my control. I totally embrace this emotion". By surrendering to the emotion, that emotion is fully embraced and released. Providing crying is done with hindsight afterwards, then crying can be a very powerful form of release. Harbouring control is one of the reasons that causes us much pain. For when we control, we resist, and when we resist we create dis-ease in the mind, body and spirit.

Of course, this doesn't mean that we should all start crying over our problems! Instead it is a message that many of us need to hear, for we have all been subject to situations where we are faced with crying to ourselves. If an emotion is building up and you feel that you could cry but you are holding yourself back for fear of looking weak, even to yourself, then think again! Too often, we control every part of our lives, including our emotions, and this causes us even more stress. Crying is a time of complete surrender. It is a very brave act, for you are letting go of your attachments to all and surrendering to the moment – whether it be that emotion or not. On an energetic level, you are releasing that emotion after embracing it and are undertaking a valuable psychological process. After the moment of release, use your awareness to look back at what you have just felt, not from a place of weakness or guilt for having just cried but from that of a compassionate being. Understand that you have just released that emotion and now you will be able to see just how that emotion has taken a hold of you for so long. By releasing it, you have come to a place of serenity – it is much like the calm left after a storm's wake. The storm of crying leaves a peacefulness and here you can use your awareness to look at yourself compassionately – Love yourself. See that this is simply an emotion. It is simply a movie that you have written. Relax. Unwind and take flight again.

As we learn to acknowledge our negative emotions, we learn to face our Dark side more and more and realise that it is a part of us. You are All Things. You are the Light and the Dark, the whole of existence. You are All That Is.

Shadow Side

Our shadow side is what is repressed within us – the parts of ourselves that we do not want to consciously deal with, or that we have become conditioned not to access. When you stand in the light of the sun, what do you see cast behind you? Your shadow. It is the antithesis of who you are in the Light, who you are in life, what you are conscious of – what you project. The shadow represents your unconscious – the part that you are unaware of, it is your polaric opposite. The Dark Side is what you are consciously repressing whilst the shadow is your unconscious repression.

Through the Law of Reflection, the shadow side is expressed in our outer lives. Victims attract aggressors, those more sensitive attract those more insensitive. We attract into our lives our shadow side to offer us the opportunity to reach balance, for our polarity to one extreme will inevitable cause us pain, as we are only living to one side. It is the repression of our other side (the dark side & the shadow side) that causes us so much pain. As we bring ourselves into balance and embrace our dark side, we embrace that what we have repressed.

When we look around in our lives, we see our shadow being played out. This is the beauty of the Earth plane! Your life is indeed a mirror and you will constantly be shown who you are – whether you like it or not! Your friends, colleagues, situations, lives all reflect either yourself or your shadow – making the whole of who you are. By accepting our shadow, we learn to deal with it and heal it. As mentioned in *Your life is a mirror*, we attract outside what we are feeling within through the Law of Reflection and the Law of Attraction. So, if you feel uncomfortable around certain people in your life then these people may very well be reflecting a part of your shadow. These are the parts within ourselves that are in need of love! So they are expressing themselves through the spiritual laws in order for you to see them – and heal them.

We are constantly projecting our inner selves onto our outer reality. When we are balanced, then we will mirror and magnetise those that are on our wavelength. For example, an unbalanced sensitive individual may attract extrovert individuals – there is learning for both here. For the sensitive individual, they may learn how to be more expressive and confident in their own body and Self. For the extrovert, they may learn how to become more sensitive of others' feelings and others' energies. For a balanced confident sensitive, they will attract people who do not make them uncomfortable. But don't forget that we also attract into our lives those that require healing. How do we know?! We can use ourselves as a tester – if we feel emotional discomfort from the presence of this other then we know that we have something to learn, if we do not then we know that this is another pleasant relationship!

Now let us look at a situation. Lukshmi is talking to her friend Charlotte about their days at work and then the conversation turns towards another friend they have – Jessica, whom they don't particularly like. The conversation soon becomes one that is geared towards highlighting all the bad qualities that Jessica has and fuelling each other both discuss how they cannot stand being around her, how drained they feel around her and how selfish Jessica can be.

What has occurred here? Whilst Lukshmi and Charlotte may of course have genuine reasons to be annoyed with Jessica because they are obviously feeling something – what is missing here is both these friends acknowledging that because they are *feeling* something, *it is coming from within!* We often immediately assume that when we feel something when someone else is around, it is emanating from them. However, it is us that allows this feeling and ultimately draws this feeling from within us to be felt. This is a case of projection of our shadow side. Here the two women have projected their own feelings onto Jessica, who has been used as a projection of how they are both feeling inside. The feelings of selfishness is an issue that unless Charlotte and Lukshmi have dealt with within themselves, they will find uncomfortable in another. It is when we deny traits within ourselves that we either mirror this in our outer world or we find it immediately uncomfortable when we see it in another. So selfishness is a shadow aspect of both these women, something that they have repressed and consequently find uncomfortable when they see it in another – leading to their judgement. This causes them further pain as they feel disempowered by those who are 'selfish' because they are reinforcing a subconscious belief that Jessica is in some way superior – hence their need to put her down. In order to resolve this, both women have to endeavour to see that they can be both selfish *or* maybe that they both need to be more selfish in their own lives. Once they accept this inner possibility and search their lives to see whether this may be true, they will begin the first step towards making peace with this aspect and so not find it so uncomfortable in others.

Now let us take Joshua, who enjoys multiple relationships with other women and proclaims that this makes him happy (these multiple relationships may very well do however for sake of argument let us assume that Joshua is unfulfilled in his romantic pursuits). When Joshua meets Mark (who also enjoys the same past-time) he immediately feels that he cannot stand him. This may well be something to do with a part of Joshua that may not like what he sees when he literally sees it within another individual. Often it is on a soul level and these people don't even hear about the others' antics but they immediately sense it in the other. It may be competitiveness and it may be a myriad of other things, however on some level there is a recognition of one self in the other that brings it to light, thereby making it aware, and thereby making it uncomfortable.

This is not to say that having multiple relationships is good or bad – in fact they are neither unless it is disserving us or others in some way. This is an example of *direct reflection.*

To better illustrate when we reflect the opposite, the inverse, of who we are – let us take the example of those who are generally more spirituality inclined magnetising into their world those who are more rational and material-focused. Initially there can be major battles occurring as each individual fails to perceive that the other represents their own shadow – i.e. something from which to learn about themselves! Primarily, the more spiritual individual, Beverly, may perceive the other, Larry, as a symbol of everything she despises about all things material.

Larry is an investment banker, who earns a great deal of money. He has a large house and expensive car and is always out enjoying the pleasurable sides of life through his money. Larry is very rational and doesn't have much time for those who waste time on the airy-fairy mumbo-jumbo field of spirituality!

On the other hand, Beverly, is very passionate about spirituality and is always practising her manifestations, prayers and maintains a close spiritual group of friends. When both first meet, friends take cover for fear of World War Three! Debates, arguments, insults fly across the room as each find the other everything they dislike.

What they have failed to recognise is that each represents the other's shadow. Beverly's shadow is indeed Larry as his shadow is represented by Beverly. Our first clue is our feelings – are we antagonised or harbour feelings of personal dislike towards this other individual? If so and we cannot find much compassion (understanding for why they do what they do) then this is a sign we are being faced with our shadow through the Law of Reflection. Our feelings are always a sign of, a kind of barometer for spiritual lessons.

So what is the lesson? The lesson is to recognise that through everyone there is something to learn! Especially the ones we dislike, for they represent a physical manifestation of our unconscious. By seeing within the other something that may be repressed, Beverly may see that Larry harbours aspects that her soul is actually seeking to regain balance. Although she is extremely spiritual, she has in this case, forgone the physical plane. She views all things material as unspiritual and groups money into this. Consequently, Beverly has issues with money, always in debt and never able to secure this aspect of her life. What Beverly can recognise is that we are here to balance all aspects of ourselves and that the physical plane is merely an extension of the spiritual realms. Her soul, her subconscious, has manifested this lesson through Larry, who is a very rational individual. This does not mean that Beverly needs to act exactly like Larry but she can learn something from Larry. His boundaried, grounded nature and ability to control money may be something that Beverly can take into her own life. Similarly, Larry can learn something from Beverly. Her ability to trust, have faith and surrender to the unknown may help Larry with his problems surrounding his need to control everything in his life, resulting in problems in his relationship amongst other areas. Also if Larry began to look within instead of constantly externally for his power, he may see something far grander and powerful than all the idols he has been externally worshipping his entire life.

So, as we can see, the shadow side works by revealing to us either something that we already harbour through either a ***direct reflection*** (like Mark and Joshua) or the opposite of what we are projecting through an ***inverse reflection*** (like Beverly and Larry). The saying, like attracts like & opposites attract are both true in this respect. These are in essence the Laws of Attraction and Reflection, for you are reflecting who you are, and its opposite.

Our shadows are not something to fear or repress when we encounter them or become aware of them! Far from it, your shadow is what your soul is yearning to learn about. They are also here for us to share our own unique expressions to the other. It is a sharing of experiences and understandings, so balance can be found.

Yes, it may be something you have traditionally been uncomfortable with, hence your discomfort with it within another, however remember that is because of the way you have been looking at it! Move around and see this trait from another perspective, one from loving *wise* eyes. By acknowledging and understanding it, you will transform that trait from murking in the shadows of your soul, from the depths of your unconscious to the light of your consciousness. This will then be reflected within your life as you move forwards into a greater place of happiness and confidence (self-love).

Remember, throughout your life every opportunity, is an opportunity to love. Your reflections are aspects of yourself to deeply love and accept, and to acknowledge. We are triggered by aspects that touch a certain part of ourself that we are not yet comfortable with. This is neither negative or positive, it is simply an aspect that we have yet to love. For whatever aspect is playing out, it deserves love. All aspects do. All beings do. You do.

Relationships with others provide us with the ultimate projection of our shadow side. We often do not realise but our relationships are a sign of what we are repressing and attempting to achieve (spiritual growth-wise). Have a look at your relationship(s), where have the problems been? Instead of looking at your partner or friend to blame, look within and try to understand why those qualities your partner had churned something within you? Is it because of a direct or inverse reflection? Also, remember that this doesn't undermine the feelings we harbour for those in our lives, for our feelings are very real. Instead it provides a place to explore ourselves, for we are inter-related with everything we experience in life.

Taking the victim versus aggressors example, this is very common in relationships. Not simply romantic but relationships we have with many people in our lives. Our lack of self-love, feelings of worthlessness and powerlessness force many to seek this power, this love, from others. Consequently, many become victimised by others as the victim believes that they deserve what they are receiving. Whether it is open verbal, physical abuse or unconscious victimisation, there is always a sense of powerlessness as the victim becomes locked in a cycle of pain. An inner belief that this is deserved prolongs the situation. However, it is important to recognise that victims create the reality of victimhood through the Law of Reflection. Naturally, through the Law of Attraction those that victimise others will be attracted into their reality. Of course, this is not to ignore or belittle the problem that is being experienced by those who are victimised, instead it shows that there is always the sign within. Ultimately, it is the victim that emerges much stronger from the experience once realisation is achieved, for they forgo their suffering as well as transforming their feelings of unworthiness into true inner confidence, something that is formidable.

GUILT, JEALOUSY & ENVY

Guilt is a fear-based emotion.

Guilt attempts to maintain its notion that we are separate from one another in the belief system that we 'owe' one another things. It is the Ego's way of rationalising pain and our sensitivity to others' pain. This is because the Ego believes that we are separate!

In reality, pain is simply there to be brought out because it must have been there to be exposed in the first place. Pain helps us grow and whenever there is pain, it is an opportunity manifested by the Being in question for self-growth.

Guilt serves no one. It is a negative emotion that traps many with its repetitive cycle within the mind. Guilt can trap one into the past and drastically affect one's present and future. Ultimately guilt inhibits an individual from growth.

Guilt blames us for our actions. It is a form of self-pity. In any given situation, where guilt is involved, we swap from feeling sorry for ourselves to blaming ourselves and fail to see what the lesson really is. We fail to see that the situation was merely present to highlight an area in our life that needed healing.

This is why it is essential to look at our life from a subjective point of view. When we see with our eagle eyes, with our angel eyes, we see every situation as an opportunity for growth – we become less judgemental of how we acted and instead we concentrate on *why* we acted this way. Then we can heal that situation and prevent ourselves from repeating the pattern.

Guilt is the Ego's way of cementing ourselves into the past. It is the emotional way in which we become locked into cycles of anguish and remorse over our past actions and manifestations. Remember, the past is always changing, according to *your* perceptions, no one else's.

Harbouring feelings of guilt limits your freedom to BE. Let us take a common example. Let's say that we feel obliged to visit our parents every now and then, or that we feel obliged to spend more time with our parents. We may feel that we have busy lives and do not have time for them, or we feel that we regress when we encounter them and feel trapped! We then find ourselves being blunt and rude in their presence when we do visit them. As soon as we part company, we feel that we have not made the effort to be nicer and calmer and we realise that our parents simply want to spend time with us. Bang. Guilt enters the scene. We feel guilty for not having acted a certain way. This is very common, not simply with parents but with relationships with friends, strangers and partners. We often feel guilt for not having acted certain ways or having done certain things. If we look deeper we see that *guilt resides from a reasoning that we have allowed others to suffer*.

This is where we can effectively see that this reasoning is flawed. We are assuming that we hold the power to make someone else suffer. Yes, this can be true if this is our intent to make someone suffer. So how do we know? *Guilt is the sign that you do not desire another to suffer!* An individual that desires to harm another does not feel guilt. However, one that believes they have hurt another and is over-sensitised to their pain, does not intend to hurt people maliciously. This is where we can see the concept of guilt in an altogether different perspective. We see that in fact guilt can be used as a reminder that we are indeed wanting the best for others. It is here where we realise that we can then let go of this guilt. It serves no one. We realise that the other individual has the power to control their own happiness. By believing that we have hurt another actually makes that other individual worse! This is because we are forming the belief that we control *their* happiness. This will then support, heighten and emphasise any fears that the other individual is already harbouring about their lack of personal power and their fears of being a victim. Thus, we are in fact taking another's power energetically when we harbour guilt.

Simultaneously, we lose our own power when we harbour feelings of guilt. This is because when we feel guilty for our own actions, we are empowering the belief that we dislike our past actions. We are sending a message to our subconscious mind that we dislike our past manifestations. Therefore we are saying that we dislike a part of our-Self – the part of our-Self that acted in this way. The subconscious mind will simply hear this as "I do not like a part of my Self. I do not like my (whole) Self" and can only react by creating our outer reality where we reflect this. Remember, all of your manifestations, in the past, are moments of free will – that *you* have chosen. If we are disgusted by the way we have acted in the past then we are disgusted by a part of our-Self and we separate our-Self from our-Self! This causes us pain. And this drains our personal power.

Instead realise that you are totally free to express. If you feel that another has been hurt by your actions then realise that you have both co-created that reality. Feelings of guilt is very similar to feelings of self-pity, for you are feeling sorry for yourself for having acted that way. This will then lead you to manifest situations where you are punished. But remember it is only you who are punishing your-Self!

To combat the consuming effects of guilt, we instead turn to the power of **responsibility**. There is a misconception with the concept of responsibility. If we break down the word 'responsibility' we see that it means 'the ability to respond' to any given situation. Taking responsibility therefore means to understand and respond to our actions.

If you feel that you may have acted irrationally in a given situation, then learn from that. From this awareness you can immediately put aside the guilt and grow. Let not the guilt trample over you. Instead use your response to the situation by knowing that it wasn't done in vain. Now you have learned to not act in this same manner again. All manifestations have purpose, providing we are willing to accept this Truth.

When we feel guilt as an emotion, we must endeavour to 'nip it in the bud'. All guilt does is slow down one's life and inhibit one's growth. So instead, we transmute the emotion into an understanding of responsibility. Through practice of denying the power of guilt over us, the emotion will become less and less consuming as we begin to see it as being redundant. Then we can truly see how guilt can easily limit our entire happiness.

We soon learn to use responsibility to learn from our manifestations. We understand the situation and blame no one. Through interconnectedness we realise that people are attracted to each others' reality based on their own free will. Therefore guilt and blame are non-existent. Instead we learn from a particular situation to prevent it from repeating.

Jealousy and Envy are other such Ego-based emotions. Envy is simply a result of our Ego's fear that there is a limited amount of everything in the Universe. The Ego naturally believes that all things are finite and limited and therefore will draw in emotions of envy and jealousy because it feels that we are losing out in some way. There is in fact an infinite amount of abundance for everyone. Once we realise this, we let go of our attachments to singular events, people and situations and surrender to the miracles that lie waiting for us. Jealousy also assumes that you are inferior in some way to another – impossible! You are completely unique – *that is your power*!

If we feel an uncontrollable urge of jealousy or envy in another then it is very effective to bless this other. For when we are jealous we are empowering the belief within us that we are unable of achieving such abundance. Instead, bless the other for experiencing such abundance and happiness. Say to yourself, "I Bless him/her for their abundance. I wish them even more!" This will dramatically help both you and that other person. It will help you because it will empower the belief that you, too, are worthy of experiencing such abundance. Also it will help alleviate your fears of scarcity by reaffirming your beliefs about abundance. It will help the other energetically due to your obvious blessing. Ultimately the Universe will respond to your blessing by sending you more.

LEARNING FORGIVENESS

Forgiveness is a powerful concept that serves the one that applies it.

However, forgiveness is also a concept that has been largely misunderstood and feared. So often we have been led to believe that forgiveness means we should apologise for our behaviour or that we should allow for another's behaviour.

In fact forgiveness is a way of releasing ourselves from attachments that would otherwise hold us back. Bitterness and blame affect *us* rather than the person that it is aimed at.

FORGIVING OTHERS

Letting go of bitterness can be one of biggest challenges in life. Bitterness simply limits our reality by constantly attracting more of the same. Whenever you replay events in your mind that hold onto grudges you are empowering the belief that you have been wronged in some way. No one is wronged. By believing that you have been wronged you are empowering the belief that you will again be wronged in the future, attracting similar situations again and again. Forgiveness is not about saying "you were right or what you did to me is alright", for what happened may indeed have been painful and you may indeed have been hurt. Instead, forgiveness is about saying 'I am no longer willing to carry around the burden of these painful memories and I am no longer willing to detriment my own happiness by clinging onto negativity" – for *this* is where our pain lies.

Therefore, when we forgive we release the situation, releasing ourselves from being caged in a past event. We are saying, "OK, that was the way things were meant to be. That is exactly the way that things were meant to happen. There is purpose and perfection in everything". As soon as we make this profound statement we are freeing ourselves from the ties of guilt, blame, shame and bitterness. We are immediately reborn in this holy instant and the world is brand new for us to explore, without the ties of past events.

Forgiveness is essential for spiritual growth because it allows the soul to release negative ties and see that these negative ties are in fact lessons to be learned. If we see situations as obstacles and blame another for the way we feel, then it is us that is going to suffer by our belief that we have been hurt. Blame is the Ego's way of drawing power from a situation – that there is a winner and a loser, when in fact neither is true. Both have come together for a wonderful learning process – and both go home the winners if they see the situation in this light. *Anything* that happens to you is an opportunity for growth.

When we issue blame on others or feel guilt, we are also feeding another with our power. For example, a common scenario is that of our family. Many blame their family environment for their present conditions. For example, if a family member has constantly berated us and we blame them for things that have happened in our life, as a result of their actions, then we end up hurting ourselves even more. This is because primarily, we are saying that this family member has power over us for having been able to have affected us in this manner – we are therefore, giving our personal power away to this family member in the present. The second consequence is that we are ignoring the lessons to be learned from our experiences with this family member – maybe their berating could be used to make us stronger and our lesson could be to gather our strength and utilise it in the outer world. This ignorance of the lesson to be learned can breed a stagnation in a soul's evolution. The third consequence is that by blaming this family member we are saying that we have been wronged. The subconscious mind interprets this as 'we have been wronged, therefore we *will* be wronged' and it will instinctively manifest further situations where will be wronged again through the Laws of Reflection and Manifestation.

Forgiveness takes great courage to express, for we are battling an age old belief that we are vulnerable once we let our guard down. We have a conditioned belief that forgiving another is a weakness and it is accepting/condoning of their behaviour. This is not what forgiveness is about. Forgiveness is about understanding and compassion – it is about seeing through the eyes of your Infinite Self and seeing the greater picture. If someone has hurt you, look through their eyes and understand that people only attack when they are feeling pain themselves. The Ego reacts to pain internally by inflicting it externally, for it assumes that everyone is out to get them and pre-empts this by attacking first.

We all know that this is not the case, yet we have conditioned beliefs within us that dictate this contradiction. When we look through the eyes of our brother and sister, we see that they are simply reacting from what they know best. Remember, there are many factors to take into account, given their particular soul evolution and their sets of individual circumstances and environmental upbringings. Pain breeds fear for the unenlightened and fear breeds more fear as we well know. This is not to say that they cannot act another way, a more enlightened way – for this is ultimately their lesson – to choose *not* to inflict pain on others. However, if they fail to choose this path and have already inflicted pain, then for our benefit and for theirs it is imperative that we use compassion to deal with the situation and not our traumatised Ego's philosophy. Once we do this, we do not become attached to their power play and we release our own blockages in the process. We see the situation as a win/win scenario and we emerge feeling total release. We release our fears of the situation and we have ultimately learned our lesson, for when we release our fears we open up our reality and thus we manifest greater abundance in our own world.

Forgiveness of those that are still in our reality is one of the most difficult of all spiritual qualities to attain. When another is in your reality and persistently subjecting you to cruelty, then this requires great valour to apply the art of forgiveness. We have to learn to react less to what is being directed our way and to deflect this and realise that it *will* pass as soon as we learn to ignore it. We have to also honour ourselves to realise why we have put ourselves in this position in the first place. Can we get out of this situation? More importantly do we *want* to get out? We have to take responsibility for our manifestations. Why have we created our experiences if we actually don't like it? Do we believe we deserve to be hurt in this manner?

The Law of Attraction states that only like attracts like and the Law of Reflection states that what you feel inside will be reflected in your outside reality. Once you forgive another and say to yourself for example, "This person is feeling pain. The cruelty and harshness they inflict on me is not because of me, it is because of their own pain" then you realise and understand that you are, indeed, perfect yourself. Remember, their pain is *never* about you! It is *always* about themselves – a culmination of fears and insecurities through their life (and lives!). There is no blame of yourself or of the other as you deflect the others' directed pain. Their pain cannot last once you fill yourself with Love and feel empowered. That other person will become immensely drained as they realise that they can no longer steal your power through this way – they will be forced to find new ways of finding power and, hopefully, this person will be forced to rethink how they are acting.

If you have trouble forgiving people, visualise that the next time that you see them is their last day on this plane. See them in the light for who they are and see that they were merely acting from their own level of pain. Each and every person is totally submerged in their own pain that when they interact with others they are coming from this level of pain. So most people are acting the best they know how, with many at the whim of their Ego without even realising it. Pray that they will achieve self-awareness just as you have. Then let them go.

FORGIVING OURSELVES

When we forgive ourselves, we find meaning to our past experiences. There are lessons to be found everywhere and by acknowledging this we can spiritually grow. Forgiveness also allows us to break free of old, negative patterns that have plagued us for so long. We constantly reprimand ourselves for our actions and are too hard on ourselves.

Remember we have much to learn about ourselves and it is all part of our growth. Love *all* facets of yourself, even if they seem to cause you pain, for you know that all these facets can be enhanced through wisdom to bring you even greater qualities. If your child makes a mistake, do you punish them for the rest of their lives? No, you ensure that they learn what they have done wrong and you *continue* to love them unconditionally. Treat yourself in the same light. Berating yourself for having made a so-called mistake will only force you to linger in a perpetual state of power-loss. The reality is that there are no mistakes. Either we come out of a situation with joy and happiness or we emerge from a situation with yet another facet of ourselves that is enlightened, making us stronger and wiser – thus leading to greater happiness!

Transcending Judgement
(A Return to Innocence)

It is very easy to judge another on Earth because this plane is rich with such diversity. The Ego part of ourselves fears diversity for it represents a threat to one's own security and persona. However, as we learn to love ourselves for who we are then we do not feel threatened by others' differences. This is yet another reason that spirituality stresses to 'Love Yourself' as the root of all teachings.

By letting go of judgement we allow ourselves all the freedom in the world to act as we want and to grow as we want and also to accept others for displaying their own Truths.

Judgement is born out of our own insecurities. Each and every person views their brothers and sisters through a set of filters. These filters are built on foundations of specific and unique sets of beliefs, insecurities, opinions and feelings. Therefore, when we judge another, we are really judging ourselves.

Transcending judgement requires us to see others from a compassionate role, a higher perspective. When we realise that all our brothers and sisters are in the same boat trying to paddle home through their own sufferings, we can begin to understand the wonderful tapestry of life before us. We begin to understand that others are merely a reflection of ourselves.

Judging ourselves can be a big problem as well. We constantly berate ourselves for doing things wrong or comparing ourselves with others. This will only create more pain in our lives as we manifest this and solidify already insecure sets of beliefs within our subconscious mind. We only need to look at children to see the power of innocence. Children, with their innocent eyes, do not judge and so realise that the world is rich with excitement and unpredictability.

JUDGING YOURSELF

When we judge ourselves, we are assessing ourselves from a platform that has no foundation for growth or happiness. Judgement is in the mind of the beholder. Judgement works through an individual's beliefs, fears and insecurities to produce an opinion that will lead to yet another belief system – one where they are seen as less than whole.

We lose ourselves in self-judgment, constantly reprimanding ourselves for our actions or comparing ourselves to others. These thoughts and feelings only hurt us further and cause more anguish! Yet we seem to find it so difficult to refrain from self-judgment for our actions. Why is this?

This is because our judgments reflect a mis-understanding of what our actions actually mean. We assume that we make mistakes or say the wrong thing. These are all products of our fears and insecurities in believing that we have to act a certain way. We misunderstand what perfection means and assume that we should have, could have, would have done something differently to make a situation or experience perfect. We tell ourselves off for our past or present actions. These are all a result of conditionings and ultimately the Ego's fear of separation. Due to an internal fear of finite existence, we assume that our actions have no meaning and we try to make each one perfect.

However, judging yourself for this serves no one – it is simply a waste of time and an act that actually weakens your personal power. You will undoubtedly project your fears and insecurities through your actions or words. But remember, there are no mistakes! Everything has purpose. If you truly believe you have made a mistake or said something wrong then congratulate yourself in realising this! Take a lesson in forgiving, for it ties in with transcending judgment. Judgement reflects duality consciousness, where we have to place everything in camps of right or wrong, good or bad. Life is much more complicated than this simple dual nature of perception. Use your compassion to see the middle-path, the purpose in *all things*.

Every situation, every choice that you make is perfection. It could be no other way for it is born out of free will. All things are meant to be. This does not mean that you are a slave to fate, for the future is unset. Instead, it means that there is *meaning* behind ALL things. Every decision you make is based on the expression of your Soul. The feelings that you harbour, the beliefs that you hold, all lead to the actions that you take. When you see yourselves like this, you realise that you are but a child in the grand scheme of things. A child of the Universe.

A return to innocence is the understanding that judgement serves no one. It is the perception of seeing all your actions as that of a child, for in reality that is what you are. You are the eternal child in the playground of Eternity. There is infinite wisdom still to be learned as there is infinite awareness to be gained. See yourselves as this child. You are merely expressing in a wonderful playground that *you* built! When we look at our actions as that of an innocent, we instantly achieve growth. For it is from this viewpoint that we are able to shrug off negative emotions such as guilt, shame and blame.

When a child does something 'wrong' in our eyes, we see that the child does not mull over this act when told off. He/she simply carries on, learning from their 'mistakes'. This is due to their ability to see the world through the eyes of innocence. Innocent eyes see the world as a large, exciting place and yet has the wisdom to know that by hanging onto your mistakes you are limiting yourself and missing out. Innocent eyes do not harbour such emotions as guilt, shame, judgement and blame for they see the world as infinitely forgiving. Innocent eyes do not berate oneSelf for their actions but learn from their mistakes and jump at the next chance to prove themselves in the very same situation. Why is this?

This is because innocent eyes do not listen to their fears, to their traumatised Ego (a child's Ego has effectively not formed yet). They realise that there is nothing to be gained from mulling over a perceived mistake or in berating one-Self. Children do not see the world as judgmental, for there is no one to judge, apart from yourself. Innocence is lost when one learns to judge. However, it can be regained through awareness to give that innocence even greater meaning, one surging with wisdom.

By looking at perceived mistakes that we have done in the light of innocence and taking the wisdom from the situation, we experience the wonder of life through the eyes of the eternal child.

Judging others

"If you have one finger pointing at somebody, you have three pointing towards yourself"
Nigerian proverb

When we judge another, we judge ourselves.

Why? This is because when we judge another we are seeing aspects of another that make *us* uncomfortable. This emerges from our own insecurities and fears about these aspects within our-Self. This is born out of the Ego's fears of diversity. We fear something in another that we are already insecure about within. If one is happy with oneself then nothing can threaten those aspects of Self. When there is insecurity, however, then another's personality and actions can threaten one's own feeling of self-worth.

For example, if another is always talking about themselves and appears to be very self-centred, we may find ourselves immediately forming a judgment of this person. We might say "oh look at him, he just cares about himself, he's so ignorant of others' feelings". However, when we judge we cloud the higher purpose of why things happen. We see with the eyes of the villager on the ground instead of the one on the hilltop. From a spiritual standpoint, we can tell that this person who appears self-centred is crying out for energy from others through his constant talk about himself – he is asking for others to love him in this manner. His rudeness and ignorance of others is a result of his self-absorption and he is lost in his own sea of fears and self-analysis because he does not have much love for himself. He has constructed the theory that by continually talking about himself to others then maybe he can draw energy from others i.e. maybe others can love him.

Now we look at ourselves, for making the judgement. We have been attracted to his world and we have attracted *him* to our world – we know this much. So why have we attracted him to our world? Maybe the Universe is asking *us* to talk more about *ourselves*? The attraction could be a message from our Infinite Self to talk and care more about ourselves. We often attract those who have qualities that we want or need for growth.

Our judgements become more rigid when we see things in others that we simply do not agree with. Those who hurt others for example. It is very easy to judge such individuals because no one likes to see a person suffering especially at the hands of another. This lesson is a very difficult one and does need some patience to fully grasp. We have to accept and acknowledge that the two beings have attracted each other to the others' realities. On a soul level, we have to become aware of why this is actually important to both souls' involvement. This can include pre-life contracts, however even that cannot occur without them both agreeing to it during their lives through the Laws of Attraction, Reflection and Manifestation. Maybe to learn forgiveness or transcending control. Ultimately, we have to respect a soul's desire to grow.

This last point is very important. Taking the example of the husband and wife. Let us say that we do manage to take the aggressor out of the picture using our intervention and 'save' the victim. Here we have the unfortunate side-effects of this victim never feeling safe themselves and always feeling like they need outside protection. This example can be related to a bully at school as well. Parents know that for their child to be able to learn about independence and fearlessness, as painful as it is for the parent, the child must endeavour to stand up to the bully themselves. It is more powerful for the victim themselves to leave the situation by gathering their strength and realising that they do not have to suffer. Otherwise their child would always need protection and always feel like a victim.

However, this does not mean we stand by and let this happen! But we can help another way – through compassion. We can give this victim as much support and Love as we can. We can give them our wise loving words and compassion to help them see the situation with their angel eyes. We can affirm to them the Truth that they are not and have never have been alone, throughout all their suffering. We can endeavour to lovingly help them break free of the situations themselves. Sympathy and pity serves no one, and can have the opposite effect of making the victim feel more of a victim. However, compassion is an extremely powerful tool that works miracles for all those involved.

Of course if a situation is destructive to an individual then we do our best to take them out of the situation. However, we must endeavour to use our awareness and compassion to evaluate a situation to determine how the 'victim' will be affected by our actions – will they suffer *more* by us trying to save them?

What is crucial however is that we are honest with our judgements. Many of us believe we do not have many judgements, that we are kind, compassionate folk who understand all others. Whilst on some level this is undoubtedly true, there can be a tendency to forget that we all have judgements and this is part of the Earth experience. From the moment we are born, we begin to create judgements based on our experiences so that we may survive in the world. Our kaleidoscope vision helps us to maintain some kind of order in a chaotic place. Our loves, desires, wants, needs, opinions, emotions, experiences all converge to form our judgements, we cannot help that. Similarly, people we have never encountered before, whether they be cross-cultural or cross religious, we cannot help but judge – because how can we truly know them and where they come from until we truly understand who they are?

One example of our distortion over judgement is our tendency to see those that suffer as needing our help. This is a judgement. We are assuming that others in less fortunate situations requires us to being them to *our level*. A common example is of charitable individuals who enter countries, believing that they are saving those less civilised, those without the benefits of civilisation. It is an inherent feature of Western civilisation that deludes itself into a belief that it is superior due to its material progress. This is duality. To approach the world spiritually, we must recognise that we are each another's student just as we are a Master to another student. So be honest with your judgements – we cannot help but judge those of different races, cultures, colours, beliefs – it is natural. As soon as we recognise our judgements, we begin to break them down and raise our awareness to see higher. This is more difficult than it sounds, however we can always evaluate our judgements through the nature we interact with others. Are we using sympathy? Have we got a picture of someone else's life before we've even given them the chance to speak?

Judgement is a veil over a higher state of awareness. When we judge, we are limiting our own world because we label them as 'good' or 'bad' – more forms of duality. Instead, our plight is to transcend duality to bring in compassion.

EXTERNAL CONDITIONING
RESOLVING YOUR FILTERS

There is an old Zen story that speaks of a lion that has been brought up its entire life by sheep. From a young cub, the lion is raised to eat, drink, sleep and move like sheep. This inevitably leads the lion to believe that it is a sheep as it moves with its flock, assimilated into the collective. Then one day another lion passes by and is astonished by what it sees. So it approaches this sheep-lion and asks it to come over to a pond. Here the lion sees its reflection for the first time and true realisation sets upon it as it begins to understand who it really is.

People and society can condition us in so many ways that we become sheep to almost everything we do in our lives. We ignore our own emotions, ambitions, desires and wants because we believe that we are sheep as well. You are each that lion that has been brought up by sheep. Step out of that zone of forgetfulness and reclaim your Divine birthright as the King of Your Jungle.

Everything we do in our lives is done through a set of filters. This can be installed within us by our family, schools, institutions, religions, society, our racial background etc...The list is endless. A lot of filters are developed from childhood and through adolescence, however external conditioning still manages to program our subconscious mind with sets of beliefs. Many of us are unaware of how our filters affect our reality. It is through these filters that our subconscious creates our reality. It is through these filters that we perceive and ultimately judge everything before us. We must endeavour to ensure that any Truth resonates deep within us and is aligned with our highest truth before we allow it in.

Society's conditioning is immense. There are many 'rules' on what we should or shouldn't do. In many countries, there has been tremendous conditioning leading to the people believing that they must work 9 to 5 to pay their bills, get security, just to survive. Society frowns upon those who follow their own truths, yet it is these people that end up doing remarkably well for themselves. This is because society's thinking is based on a mass conscious fear of being separate and finite. Society's fear simply reflects our own personal fears – a macrocosm of our Ego's fear of separation. We cannot blame society anymore than we can blame ourselves! However, we can shake off society's grip through awareness. Once we change the world within, the outside world will be reflected simultaneously.

Traditional society raises its people as sheep, to think not for themselves but to be safe in the crowd where everybody else is as well. Society's fears of separateness forces its people to crowd together in fear just like sheep, to avoid getting attacked (hurt). However, the paradox in reality is that we aren't separate – we each are eternally connected to one another, yet we also each have our own Truths that make us unique. By suppressing that which we inherently are only causes us more pain. We are each born the lion, to roam and express our roar in the jungle. We are each kings of our reality and the choice is, as has always been, ours to claim. The sooner we realise this, the sooner we are free. It is up to each of us to break the cycle and be aware of what we are seeing – is it through our eyes or through the eyes of another? Society will eventually reflect our-Self-love as the peoples of the world learn to love themselves individually.

Our parents are excellent ways of seeing what is happening within us. The challenge with our parents is to merge the best qualities that they both posses to take on for ourselves as well as healing and benefiting from their combined challenges – this is spiritual growth, this is how evolution and progress is made through generations. This ultimately helps your soul evolve in a unique form of learning. We can see what conditioning our parents have put upon us and move beyond it to see that it has helped us achieve this present state of awareness. The same is true for institutions through schools, media, religions etc...

For example, a seemingly unloving parent may have helped an individual to explore their own independence than say one who experienced a blissful upbringing. Instead of seeing the negative aspects of your conditionings, see what they have given you and you will see what you are capable of – is it confidence, humour, being grounded, playfulness, a keen mind, feistiness? Remember we each chose our own birth path, environment, parents, situation, colour, country that we incarnated into. Congratulate yourselves if you have been through rough patches, for that means all the more that you have been brave enough to take on such suffering for your spiritual growth – your duties never go unnoticed. You will be rewarded in even greater form if you persevere. By seeing the positive nature in our conditionings, we transcend them through the light of our love and wisdom. Fear, of course, will only cloud a situation and breed more fear limiting our world.

Parental influences also affect how we act and interact with our partners. *Our relationship with our parents mirrors our relationship with our partners.* What we learn from our parents are role models for how we treat those we become intimate with later in life. Similarly, if we find we have difficulty finding intimacy in life then this may reflect a relationship with our parental figures where they may have abandoned us or produced feelings within where we are resentful of their behaviour or hurt. By assessing our relationships we may see a pattern that reflects a relationship with our parents. Conversely, by examining and resolving our filters with our parents we move into a space to create more loving, open and enjoyable experiences with our partners.

Group situations – *how we react in groups are a reflection of how we act within our own family.* If you find yourself always quiet in large groups or always the bossy one – check to see how you are with your own family. Are you always trying to be heard in your family? Do you find yourself doing this in groups? Or maybe you rebel in groups and are always the quiet, distant one, when in your family you are always fixing things or having to carry the burdens of other family members' problems. Our relationship to our family is paramount to how we act and interact within group environments. Of course this relates to our group of friends just as much as groups at work or elsewhere.

Our childhood and adolescence are crucial in defining what we learn and what we process, determining how we live the rest of our lives. If we carry around pains from this period, which most of us do, then this naturally will affect every single moment of the rest of our lives. Why would you want this! By beginning to look within and externally to your surroundings, begin to see patterns. See how you may be acting with your family, or your parents. Assess how much anger or pain you still carry from your childhood and adolescence. Examine what you learned from your parents. How did your parents treat you? Did you always feel loved? What might you have learned? Remember, this is not a procedure in blaming our parents or family for anything, for there is something to learn and grow from every experience. Instead, it is necessary to better understand ourselves – if we are to transform our insecurities within our relationships and group environments to powerful strengths.

Let us look at Frank, a successful city worker. Frank has had trouble maintaining stable relationships and usually jumps from one to another. At first he enjoyed this experience of meeting new partners however after a while he has become despondent about his predicament. He feels it better to be alone and lives most of his adult life single and care-free. Looking back into Frank's early life, we see that both of Frank's parents are very successful professionals. Frank's parents were such dominant, over-powering individuals that whenever Frank vied for their attention he was shunned as his parents were extremely busy. Now children usually go two different ways here – some act out in order to get the attention they desperately need through rebelling and becoming totally uncontrollable. However, Frank went the other and created the theory that the only way he could achieve autonomy was through isolation. Here, Frank maintained himself to himself and with no other siblings, this proved to work on some level for him. Of course, this theory forms the bedrock of Frank's kaleidoscope vision. His adult life is but an extension of his adolescence, which itself but an extension of his childhood. Frank's isolated nature has developed into a fear of intimacy as well as a fear that he may be rejected if he tries to get close again.

Another example is if a parent has highly opinionated views on the opposite sex, then this filter may be taken on by the child who naturally views their parent as their role model. The child may then grow up to attract members of the opposite sex who fit his/her perceptions and beliefs.

Our parents are wonderful teachers of who we are. Remember, that parents were once children themselves and experienced whatever events and situations they experienced to make them who *they* are. We are all a result of our conditionings and inner theories.

THE BOX SYNDROME

To break away from conditionings, we need to understand how and why they affect us. When others have judgements or opinions of your character they are energetically feeding off fears about yourself. Insecurities that you feel all fuel any negative perceptions of your character that others may harbour. This then, of course, places you into a box, where others expect you to act in certain ways and feel certain things. This box can be difficult to break out of. To do this, one needs to develop the strength of character to deflect others' opinions and judgements. However, this strength of character does not require years of self-help, it simply requires trust and faith that by breaking out you are doing yourself a favour. Faith is where all strength is born.

Breaking out of the box requires us to completely change the way we perceive reality.

See less through the eyes of your brothers and sisters and stay in the Truth that is your own. Becoming immersed in other people's movies and their opinions of yourself only deters you from your own Truth. You are your-Self. There is no other like you, nor could there be.

EXPRESSING YOURSELF & SELF-ACCEPTANCE

Why does it matter what other people think of you?

This is deep rooted in an insecurity of self-acceptance. We all want to be accepted and when we strive to be liked and accepted we tend to do what other people want or act how we *think* other people want. Here, we fail to realise that by acting against our true expression to suit the lives of another only creates pain for ourselves.

When we express ourselves we are BE-coming ONE with our True Self – we ignore the movies of others. Then we magnetise all those who are in sync with our desires and loves.

RELATING TO OTHERS

We so often get caught up in other people's movies and act in a way that will please them. This is not only an insecurity of wanting to be liked but also a *power reaction*. By assuming that these people will like us for acting a certain way, we assume that they will send us their power (love) and thus comfort us. However, we must realise that the only power (love) we ever need or that will ever satisfy us is that from ourselves. Once we are happy with ourselves and who we are, then no matter how we act we cannot be harmed from the external world.

How often do you say to yourself, 'I should act like this or I should be more like him or her'. This is truly the hurt Ego/fearful part of your-Self speaking, for anything that limits you is not you! You are by essence infinite, wondrous powerful playful beings of pure energy. Any thought within you that tells you to act a certain way, immediately recognise it as being not of Love and deny it entry into your Being.

Persona Projection

Throughout every part of our life, we desire to belong, we desire to be part of something, we desire to fit in – ultimately we are desiring to be liked.

When we meet others and adapt our personalities, we are doing so in an effort to be liked, to be accepted by these others. However, what we are actually doing is informing our subconscious mind that we don't think our real self is worthy of people's attention or liking. We are basically telling ourselves that we are unworthy as we truly are and therefore must act like another. This obviously creates the internal theory that we are inferior and that we do not love ourselves, manifesting this in all parts of our life.

We fear that others may reject us for who we really are, so we use a shield. This shield is often a *persona projection* that we emit to others in an effort to protect our true self. We use others as examples of how we believe we should act, in order to be liked. We theorise that he/she is popular, therefore I must act like them to be liked. Our persona projection changes constantly as we attempt to find the right person to project in order to be liked by others.

We project an image of what we want others to see and how we like to be seen. Much of this image comes out of inner insecurities of being afraid of projecting our real feelings and persona. This is not just born from childhood and adolescence but also from external conditioning of how we are supposed to act in society. Many of us feel compelled to act differently around different people, whether it be because certain people react differently to certain things or whether we are just trying to get along or please them. Again this is all to do with wanting to be liked.

We are all expert intuits, we have simply forgotten this. When we meet people we can tell what their likes and dislikes are and many of us are either subconsciously or consciously adapting our personalities to suit those before us. This is really a cry out saying, "Hey, love me!" As naturally loving beings who do not love ourselves we will endeavour to find this love wherever we can. We desperately want to be accepted by everyone, everyone we meet, every single person we encounter. We tell ourselves that we don't care if people don't like us, yet deep down no one likes not being liked. We want to be accepted by everyone…yet we do not first look at the main person that is not accepting ourselves…us! In order for others to accept who we are, we must first ourselves be comfortable with who we are! This seems such a simple concept, yet most of us have such difficulty in acknowledging and utilising it. We constantly look externally but we are still not going to the root of the problem , which always comes from within. Because everything comes from within! Endeavour to realise the beauty, splendour, grace, power, magnificence, truth, love that is your-Self. There is not one other being like you. You have something to offer that no other person can. You have unique personality traits that no other person has to the same degree. The love that you seek from others will come as a reflection of the love you have for ourselves, as opposed to the other way round. We are still seeking others to love us so that we may feel good about ourselves rather the other way round. Yes it is much harder this way round!

Others cannot provide us with happiness because their love will constantly be fluctuating, as it is their right to do so. So when their love for us changes, we immediately become upset. However if we are centred and empowered with the love and acceptance we have for ourselves, then whether others' love for us changes or not is irrelevant. We do not even notice! Because we feel confident, secure, empowered, loved from within. We do not rely (therefore depend) on others and become more and more confident with each step we take, each act we make, each thing we say.

When we find ourselves in situations where we feel threatened by the personalities of others or feel inferior in some way, we know for certain this is an insecurity on our part. We must endeavour to realise that this other person isn't as glorified as we like to make them! They may not seem as happy as we like to believe, this is just an illusion. In any case, it is irrelevant whether this other person is happy or not, this is just a way of understanding that our perception of what they are is just that – a perception. Our insecurities will glorify anyone who believe to be better than us, in the end we realise that anyone else can never be compared to who we are. The more we compare ourselves, the more we refrain from being ourselves, the more insecure we feel and the less we express – ultimately we become what we fear – shy, insecure and afraid.

However, we must realise that to seek this love externally we are denying who we are and thus propagating our situation further. For, if we seek to be accepted externally, we will continue to seek external validity because that is where we believe it to reside! However, when we validate ourselves internally, the external world becomes our playground and one we can explore into and not be fearful of. We do not fear rejection because we are fully accepted within.

Our internal psychology will create theories upon theories of our dislike for ourselves and this will affect every thought, decision, action and feeling in our lives. The more we act out of character, out of personality, the more we reinforce this internal theory and the unhappier we become. Consequently, we transmit this notion to those around us. Others sense our inherent dislike for ourselves and the way we act and we become more and more distant from our original intention – of wanting to be liked!

When you truly accept everything that you are, you love all aspects of yourself – therefore you do not need another to love or accept us in order to feel worthy. You are then free to be yourself as acceptance comes from within, giving you total freedom to BE. By being true to yourself, you are doing a far greater service to yourself and to the mass consciousness, which is naked without your unique, self-expression. You have a unique persona to express, this all adds to the greater consciousness of understanding everything. By holding back, we are not helping anyone especially ourselves. Look deep within and see what projections you put out in the company of certain people and see the true personality within you. When you honestly act in alliance with your True Divine Self, people cannot help but be in awe because it will resonate within them that you are being yourself.

Being ourselves is one of the most difficult things we can do. This is because inherently, we do not love ourselves and so we inform ourselves that no one actually likes who we are! Why would anyone like us for being ourselves?

REJECTION

So what is rejection? It is a fear of another not accepting you, liking you. In essence it is a mixture of attachments and self-acceptance. Here, it is a need for external validation that results in the fear that this may be taken away – that our attachment (outsourcing to an externality, in this case people) may be stricken. We all fear or experience rejection in many parts of our lives – yet it is how we approach rejection that completely transforms the idea of being rejected into something far different, into something where we are actually learning something. Ultimately it becomes a gift, for it is showing ourselves another part of ourselves that is requiring love and attention – thus we are able to heal that part and move forward with renewed confidence.

Let us take an example. The first example is that of a man who has been rejected by his partner. Now the Ego's power struggle theory will of course dictate that he has lost – lost power. Indeed, if he was outsourcing his power from his partner then he would lose this power – and the feeling of rejection would be significantly felt – a loss of power, hurt, rejected i.e. not feeling wanted, liked – loved. And so we see the lineage that leads to this feeling of not being loved, this of course reflects this man's inner lack of self-love. When we do hot harbour a love for ourselves then we of course attach this to externalities, in this case people. When our externality changes, in this case the other person shifts, so does this man's source of power (love). He is left feeling powerless, empty, rejected. However the rejection becomes the gift. Here, the rejection allows this individual to finally recognise the truth of who they are. For before this situation he has been acting *out of his character* in order to be loved. He is outsourcing his power and his personality! In truth he must ask himself whether he truly knows himself, and therefore how can his partner? Also how can he truly know who is partner is – if he is first seeing life through his own filters and then his partner is a projection of his own wants/desires!

From one perspective, both are seeing projections of their own illusions of who they think the other individual is. Both projections are of course filtered through their own insecurities and their own experiences. This is not to say that there is no love, for all are beings of love who act in ways that serve love. However, who is being truthful to who they are? All of these result from the lack of self-love each has for themselves. This man has been given a Divine Gift – a chance to finally see who he is. As he feels rejected, it allows him to finally look at himself and his actions, the *time* to reflect. It is here, it is within these crucial moments of self-analysis and seemingly self-hatred, comparison and feelings of inferiority that he know has the chance to redeem his power. And what is power but love. When we goes to that place within himself, he shines light into his dark and sources unconditional love from within himself.

When they truly become themselves, then they radiate their presence in all directions. Those that they meet will resonate to *who they are* as opposed to what they are trying to project for others to like. This of course is a very different energy.

We spend so much of our time pretending to be something we are not, only to realise that being who we are is what can only make us happy – and those who truly resonate with us – leading to exponential growth and joy.

Of course all reality is a result of the law of attraction and reflection and we are reflecting our insecurities in those around us and then attract them into our reality! So this case involves both individuals co-creating a situation where one is left feeling rejected by the other – inviting tremendous spiritual growth for both if awareness is used. There is no blame here for either individual, only a powerful, magical opportunity for each to act as a catalyst for each other to then proceed on their paths of truly being and living their Divine Expressions.

The second example is that of a woman who has just joined a company and encounters what she perceived as a tight clique of workers. Here she finds it difficult to fit in. what is happening here? Against this relates to self-acceptance. This woman is afraid that she may not be accepted by the whole (the group of existing employees). Here she finds it difficult to fit in. She fears rejection – so that even when she make friends with her co-workers, she has grouped them as a whole that is separate to her. What is important here, what is highlighted is how her fear *of* rejection, of a future pain has determined her present action. She has limited herself, and caused herself pain by fearing a possible future scenario.

BEING YOURSELF

Being our-self requires us to constantly express who we truly are all the time. If we are constantly adapting to others when we feel threatened or we want to be liked, we know the reason – we want to be liked! If you find yourself doing this in front of your boss, your parent, your friends, these are signs you are acting out of character – therefore you are acting out of your own truth and are therefore only causing yourself harm. By acting out of character, it empowers beliefs that you are inferior.

If you sense that others at first do not like your change, you must endeavour to ignore this restrictive feeling – for in reality it is not emanating from others, it is stemming from your own Ego. it is your divine birthright to be yourself. There is not another that can be like you. By being yourself, you are God expressing him/herself. This is one of the hardest lessons to learn but one of the most rewarding at the same time. This is because it allows us to be free. We are at our most free when we are acting like our true self. Be yourself, lose the effort and relax into life, into existence, into the joy of living. Living with joy comes through ease. Be yourself, it will set you free.

Every time you feel afraid of being rejected for acting like yourself, or not like another, remind yourself – this is just a fear of my own rejection. I accept myself.

So let us examine why we feel that we can't act in certain ways. We often feel that we feel so restricted in the way that we act. However, who is doing the restricting here?! It is you! There is not one other person that can make you express or restrict you. You allow your own expression, so why is there difficulty in expressing? This is because of course a fear of self-acceptance. Is this other going to accept me? Is this other person going to accept or reject who I truly am? The fundamental point here is that the real rejection and the real self-acceptance here is being done on our side. It is completely irrelevant what another thinks of us - why? Because we cannot really outsource power (love) from others.

Opinions are constantly changing according to their own ever-changing state of mind. So why establish, root your power, your security within something that is so unpredictable? This will ensure your insecurity!

You also empower an internal belief that you need that other, empowering further negative beliefs (insecurities) It is far more potent to your power to draw that power, that love, from within. Then you ensure you own security - expand.

So the next step is of course, understanding how to self-express. This as with all positive traits must be first done through awareness. i.e. we cannot simply begin self-expressing with confidence if we are not aware of why we are not being confident in the first place! This is easier than it sounds. When you limit your true self-expression, you are basically sending yourself a message. That message is that you do not believe that your self-expression is worthy of others to hear, see or interact with. But, let us look deeper. Here we see that it is first us that claims we are not worthy before others even have the chance of making that decision! So it is the root where we must target and transform if we are to transform ourselves. In reality, everything comes down to how we feel about ourselves. In order to target this we need to begin to understand just how crucial it is to learn to love ourselves if we are to be happy, confident and enjoy life with freedom. Full self-expression is the freedom we desire. You are inherently every positive trait that you could possible desire - you are All That Is. You have all the confidence, security and happiness within, for you are perfection and total power.

In order for us to reach that state, and this doesn't take a year of therapy or a dozen self-help books to get to. This is because we already harbour these positive traits within us, we have simply taught ourselves that we are insecure, shy and inferior to others. Or we have allowed others to teach us, which in reality is US allowing those others, US believing those others - so always it comes down to us.

"When you were born, you cried and the world rejoiced. Live your life so that when you die, the world cries and you

rejoice"
Cherokee proverb

Today, imagine that it is your last day on earth – what would you like to do? Take a look at your Self-expression. You can act like you want and not be harassed by should's and shouldn'ts from your traumatised Ego or external conditioning. Isn't this thought freeing? Now realise that each day is your last day because as soon as it passes, it becomes the past! Do not fret over the past for this moment is all that exists. This is why it is so important to live in the NOW. You can do anything you want and it shouldn't take an apocalypse to help you realise this!

We say to ourselves, "Oh I really want to act like this but I don't know how these people will react" – but we fail to fully analyse our thought process. For if we continued we would realise that what we are really thinking is: 'I want them to accept what I'm about to do or say and I don't want to be rejected or ridiculed for my change in self-expression.' It is the change that breeds fear because subconsciously we know that other people fear change as well! We fear a possible rejection in reaction to our change, for we have outsourced our power – we know others . However, if we turn that around and act from the knowledge of Love rather than fear, we can now say that we are all children of the Divine, we are all connected and we are all reflections of the One, therefore whatever I do, whichever way I act, I am doing a service to my fellow beings for showing them another aspect of themselves. No one judges us as harshly as we judge ourselves. Who is to say this is right or wrong, for nothing is right or wrong – this is more duality consciousness. Each being's expression is a unique song that releases a unique melody. To take away one of those songs disrupts the entire orchestra of the Whole. This is how important you are.

By being aware we can see the barriers that exist around our personality traits. This can be external conditioning or internal – it all comes down to fear of change. It comes down to listening to the Ego which states, "Don't take a risk. Don't try and be different, others will notice and judge you." Let us break this down. What the Ego is actually saying is 'if you change the status quo, you make life unpredictable and unstable and I'm scared of this because then I don't know if others will still give me their power (love).'

Our fear of judgement is really a reflection of us judging ourselves, for how we believe another can judge us is a projection of our own self-judgement. Break free of this self-confinement! You are the only person that judges you!

First we must accept ourselves for who we are, irrespective of who anyone else is. We must endeavour to realise that as a unique being, we have a unique song (expression) needed to provide the unique melody created by the chorus of the whole. This speciality, this uniqueness is essential because we are not attempting to become like another to be accepted. As we realise this fundamental truth, we begin to accept the truth of who we are.

Ultimately, we are accepting ourselves. this is crucial for us to function in life because everything we do is irrevocably influenced by how we feel about ourselves.

Through self-acceptance, we come to a place where the external world completely changes from how we viewed it before. Instead of being a place of need, the external world becomes are true playground. This is because where before we were seeking external validation and love from others, the external world was a place of fear, where we could easily be rejected, be hurt, be pained in some way as others do not accept who we are and ultimately love us. However, when we source that acceptance, that power, that love from within, the external world is not a place that we need anything of the sort. Instead it truly becomes an arena where we can express the totality of our being, the beauty and uniqueness of our soul for all those to see. We are free.

Here, we see all people as unique and accept others in the most ultimate way possible – we have love for all people for who they truly are as well.

It is our inherent uniqueness that allows us to be. It is our uniqueness that provides the freedom for us to be who we truly are. When we are being ourselves, we are free, we are not limiting ourselves in any way. We are not restricting ourselves. When we restrict, anything for that matter, are limiting. When we are limiting, we are limiting our world, for we are setting boundaries on how we act – thus living where we are controlling who we are. Control, limitation, restriction are all assets of misery because these are very draining forms of existence.

When we are controlling who we are, we spend a lot of energy trying to be someone else other than who we really. For when we are truly ourselves, there is complete effortlessness in just being. By trying to be another, we spend a lot of energy, which becomes stress, in being something we are not and worrying whether we are acting out of the character (persona projection) we have created. Being someone we are not is very difficult and takes a lot of energy! Yet most of us do this most of the time.

As we endeavour to express our uniqueness, we attract others around us like a magnet. This is because we are shining our Light from within. It is the paradox of life that we look up to those who express their true selves and wonder why can't we do that, yet we respond by acting like that person we admire! This reasoning is founded on the belief that – they are accepted for who they are, so if I act like them then I will be accepted and loved as well. Of course, this reasoning is illogical yet we find ourselves again and again falling into this trap as we attempt to find our connection to others.

Our true connection of course, is the connection within.

BREAKING FREE OF THE BOX

If you find it hard to express yourself with people and find that you are overtly self-conscious of everything you do – first start by seeing the people you know as strangers. This is because many of us become shaped by what our friends, family and loved ones expect us to be (external conditioning). Have you noticed when you are on holiday or meet someone new you can act how you want? When we are around people our whole lives, we tend to be placed in a box of how we are supposed to act. When we act outside of this box, people become shocked and this is one of the reasons why many feel trapped from re-inventing themselves. The other reason is of course we are afraid that others will judge us for our change. The truth is that life is about constantly re-inventing yourself, so that you may grow and become more than you were yesterday or the year before. Take time apart to yourself so you may see deep within you, what it is you want to change and then change it.

For those who feel particularly personality boxed, it may be prudent to assess their personal relationships. This does not mean you have to leave your friends and find new more-lovingly allowing souls! (Although if you want, this is a perfectly valid choice as well). Instead, it means that we can assess how our personal relationships are affecting our lives – are they limiting us in more ways that we realise? This is an important question, because many do not realise the external conditioning that they are umbrella'd under. One of the reasons people are attracted to travelling independently for a while is that it allows them the opportunity to travel free of these external conditions on their personality. The freedom is exhilarating. We have so many aspects of our personality that lie dormant, waiting for us to access and embellish them. Friends, family and loved ones can see you in a certain way and soon you see yourself in that way and fear breaking that tradition.

Of course, we do not need to travel to the ends of the earth to gain this freedom! Nor do we have to find new friends! We can begin wherever we are by claiming our life as our own. This takes courage but it is *your* life. It is your birthright to act and feel as you desire. You have free will. You have the ability to create. You can choose to say 'yes' and 'no.'

You have all the facets of *all* the personality traits that you desire – for everyone is simply a reflection of You. Those you envy for being more confident or for seemingly possessing whatever quality that you desire, *know* that you too have this ability and much more. You can seize any part of your whole personality whenever you desire. While it is true that we each incarnate in life with particular personality traits, what we desire and how we surface new personality traits is the whole process of soul growth. We have all seen others making huge strides in their self-expression. A shy child at school becomes a famous actor – this is not an uncommon story. See yourself as the lotus flower, forever unfolding and blossoming as your Self-expression explores wonderful new possibilities.

Ignore primitive urgings of your traumatised Ego and move beyond it into the knowing that you are truly brave. Instead, let your Inner Child free to play in the arena of your imagination. Others will see your bravery in self-expression and it may prompt them to open up more. Even if others do label you as doing something embarrassing or out of the norm, they will think about it for five minutes then carry on with their own lives. They will soon become self-absorbed within their own world. However, the important thing here is to not let others' judgments affect our own lives. Who are we living for then? For them or for us? It is imperative for our own happiness that we *be* ourselves and explore ourselves. When we live for others, to keep others happy – how can *we* be happy?

Know that by breaking free, you are making the first steps to greater freedom and attracting all the more abundance than was previously available. You also refine your connections with your creative abilities and inspiration, which thrive on self-expression. You empower your subconscious with more expansive beliefs for manifestation. Ultimately your-Self-confidence (your-Self-love) will increase to whole new levels.

Remember you are constantly reborn each and every minute. You have the eternal choice each passing moment to BE all the more than you were the moment before. Do you take this golden ticket to freedom and happiness?

BE anything that you desire, dance the living fire that is your Heart. When you act out of Self and ignore the Ego's cravings for external validation then you expand the Self and embrace true limitless possibilities. This then affects the laws of manifestation – once you feel free, by laws of attraction you will bring into your life the truly magnificent scope of abundance that is readily available to you.

Be yourself. You are far more powerful by drawing on your inherent unique strengths than you could possibly realise. It is when we align our state of being with our inner Truths that we excel and radiate such powerfully magnetic Divinity that all are attracted to our world, in awe of the way we live.

When we turn our heads upward and outward and embrace the truly awe-inspiring limitless scope of eternity that is our Self-expression, we can achieve anything. When we let go of our outdated modes of beliefs of limited conditioning, we can establish a rock-solid foundation of Love to build our-Self from. We can brush away the negative thought patterns that have imprisoned our Heart Self from creatively expressing itself and truly be invulnerable in the knowledge that whatever we do in each moment is another expression of the Divine.

RESPECTING YOURSELF

Respecting oneself is something that most of us have great difficulty in achieving. You've heard the saying, "If you don't respect yourself, how can you expect others to respect you?" What does this actually mean? It means that having respect for oneself means that we understand our self-worth. Feelings of worthlessness are paramount in restricting our experiences and happiness. Respecting yourself of course is dependent upon loving yourself. Do you love yourself? Do you *really* love yourself?

Resilience allows us to respect ourself as it provides one alternate way of viewing ourselves. Resilience allows you to stand in your own truth along with a tide of the Truths of others. It is the *knowing* that you *are* Truth, prevailing. It prevents you from becoming immersed with other people's emotional luggage and helps you from getting umbrella'd under other people's opinions of how you should be. It is the embodiment of expressing who YOU are - the unique YOU, resilient to all external restrictions – your inner You. Resilience is being able to break free from limiting situations and standing your ground for your personal Truth, irrespective of 'opposition'. When you are truly resilient, you express your Truth in such a loving way that others will flock towards it as you magnetise those on a similar wavelength.

Remember it is your prerogative to be who you are.

To practice resilience involves listening less to other people's emotions, dramas, judgements, feelings and movies and more to your own inner drive, voice, meaning and truth. Many are overly sensitive and act like a television, trying to juggle a hundred channels but losing sight of where their own channel resides! The more you practice what you preach, the more you learn to live by it.

We tend to allow other people's movies to control our decisions due to power-based attachments or due to our over sensitivities to what people think of us. Why let another take your limelight! This is *your* stage, you are the central figure of your world.

Learning to de-tach ourselves from emotionally charged situations is one of the key factors to gaining our freedom and developing our resilience [see Attachments for further study]. Begin to observe negative energy rather than reacting to it. Sensitive souls often suffer from becoming too emotionally involved in situations and can lose a lot of their power this way.

For example, if someone personally criticises you, it is very easy to become attached to this statement and ignore all the positive statements people have previously said about you! Fear is contagious. So initially we *stop*. Be Still. Relax, for you *know* that you cannot be harmed unless you allow it. Let not their negativity become a part of your response, for you will be pulled into their world of negativity and it will become part of yours. Also remember that it is your creation, through the Law of Reflection – so why does it hurt you – is it a challenge because it highlights something you already feel or is it something to overcome by standing your ground? Just as fear is contagious so is Love. Be strong in the Truth of who you are in your essence – you are GOD, nothing less. Repel negative statements, allow them to graciously glide over your magnificence. Things can only hurt you if you *allow* them to hurt you. The ball is always in your court. Know that others are being criticised by other people, just as you, but the ones who are resilient and do not let it affect them are the ones that repel this energy.

Too often, we react to another's hurtful actions towards us by attacking ourselves. Know that those who hurt others are experiencing pain in their lives just like everybody else, they just deal with it differently. Send them love so that they may become aware of their pain and deal with it effectively and quickly. Smile an inner smile, for *you know* that the wisdom of your Light is far more powerful. This act can truly help them, on an energetic level, if they are unwilling to listen to your wise loving words.

Being overtly self-conscious is another barrier to Self Love and another need for resilience. This is a mirror of our insecurities. You are perfect as you are – Be Yourself. By looking through someone else's eyes you have just left your reality and become part of that person's energy system. It works both ways – be aware of other's energy but don't get lost in their movies! Break free of the reins of conditioning, both external and internal and let loose the warrior within you. You have all the freedom in the world at your very fingertips, it has and always will be, Your Choice.

Learn to laugh at yourself in situations when you find yourself normally attacking yourself for having done something regrettable. Let's take embarrassment for example. Embarrassment, if we break it down, is simply a fear of acceptance – we fear breaking out of the reins of conditioning and the boxed personality that others and ourselves have placed upon our Being. When we act out of character with that 'stereotype' of how we 'should act' – we become fearful of acceptance. Our Ego tells us "this isn't how you're supposed to act!" What it's really telling us is that when we act outside of our box we become less secure in drawing in our power from others. This is why our Ego thrives on security – for in stable environments, it knows where it can get power from and is unthreatened by change.

Once we realise that we are free to express as whomever or whatever we desire, we truly open up our personality for growth. Remember yourself five years ago, how much have you changed? Now realise that you can change constantly, why wait five years to try something new? When you look at someone else and desire a personality trait – you already have that trait within you! For they are merely a reflection of you. If you want to be more joyful or confident or energetic – you can do this! The key is breaking free of the reins of conditioning through faith. As with all things that lead to freedom, this takes courage. If you are willing to be brave for yourself, then you will be rewarded infinitely. Have you noticed how you admire people who can freely express themselves *in spite* of embarrassment? If we label ourselves as simply being 'shy' then we are limiting ourselves. We are ALL capable of Full Self-Expression.

FOLLOW YOUR OWN TRUTH

The enlightened person is one who challenges others to be courageous enough to take responsibility for who they are and to live their truth. Following your Truth and standing your ground requires you to build your personal power to such an extent so that nothing or no-one can deter you off your path. You will meet many obstacles from those who fear what they see in you – for there will be others who are too used to being locked in misery in their pens. Misery as negative as it is, still provides a security for those who are fear-based. Show them the Light by *Following Your Truth*.

Remember that we are offended by things that are not ours in the first place – external conditioning in the form of beliefs, power, anything related to fear. For when we truly believe in something, we cannot be offended and do not feel we have to defend ourselves because we know we are right in our-Self. Being offended comes from a power struggle initiated by the Ego, where the Ego feels that someone is attacking our beliefs and our security. In essence all beliefs are essentially unstable because they represent categorised forms of faith. Anything unwilling to change will cause us pain. When we hold all our power in ourselves and in love i.e. evolving truths, then nothing can offend us for we know that all is allowed. It is the Knowing that allows us to be at peace.

For many of us, it is also important to learn to say 'no'. This is another cultural conditioning that teaches us that when we say no, we are being selfish or hurting the feelings of another. We are hurting ourselves more by doing this! Be strong for there will only be regret when you accept to do something or agree to something that you do not truly desire. When we find it difficult to say 'No' we are doing two things. First we are sending a clear message to that other person, saying "I'm saying yes because I want you to love me! If I say no, then this might threaten your love for me!" Second we are sending a clear message to ourselves that we need others to make us happy and to make us feel good about ourselves. This obviously empowers the subconscious belief within us that we are unloved and that we cannot stand up for ourselves, manifesting more situations of being forced into the victim role.

Many find it hard to grasp the act of saying 'no' because they are clouded by outmoded patterns of thinking such as guilt. This is the Ego telling you that there can only be a winner and a loser to the situation. Yes, others can experience pain from us saying, 'sorry, no, actually I don't want to do that. I want to do this instead'. But we have to assess "is their pain in response to a power struggle loss of their own Ego or is it because we are being rude!" If we are loving in our response then we know that we are simply following our Truth and they are feeling the pain brought on about by their own Ego. We can send them Love and leave them on their path but it is very important for us to Follow our Truth. We have to respect ourselves and see with our eagle eyes that they themselves have a lesson to learn that others can follow their own Truth if they wish.

Happiness can only come from within you, for it is always you who determines what makes you happy! If you are true to yourself, others will Love you even more not less! It might take some a longer journey to realise this but eventually they will admire your resilience and honour of yourself and will follow suit themselves.

You can be strong and stand up for yourself in a supremely loving way – you can state your truth in an almost amusingly royal way, others cannot but accept your truth when you state it with love and joy. Break free of the reins. Your Freedom is HERE.

Remember that each and every single person is an expression of the Divine. To deny what you feel and to disallow your Truth is to deny the Universe within.

RADIATE WHAT YOU RESONATE

The Universe experiences through you, the Oneness experiences through your expressions. When you express your Truths, no matter what they are, you are adding to Universal Consciousness. When we repress that which is within us we deny All That Is.

Let us take an example. Those who seem to attract others with over-powering personalities feel trapped yet do not like to tell them to back off for fear of hurting their feelings. What we must realise is that by allowing others to constantly invade our personal space or talk about themselves, making us feel trapped, is only hurting both of us simultaneously. When we speak out our Truth, and say what we truly feel then it will always be in the best intentions of both parties involved. (See Embracing Your Dark Side on dealing with informing others of our pain with them).

If you do not respect yourself, how can that be mirrored back to you? How can others respect you in the same way? You must endeavour to live your life with such passion that you truly radiate your individual expression. Some people may view this as selfish but they, themselves, will eventually come round and realise the Truth in this. Within each of you is an eternal flame of your Truth, feel this resonate within you and radiate it out to the world. Your truth is so important for the rest of the world that it is precisely why you have incarnated here – to express it. Your life is yours to claim. Reclaim your right to Live!

Releasing Responsibility for Others

It is important to honour your own power. Sensitive souls feel particularly drawn or tied to those who harbour feelings of self-pity. The result is feelings of guilt within when we feel we aren't helping others enough, have said/done something to upset them or 'feel' for their pain. Here we must endeavour to release responsibility for how others feel around us. We are not responsible for the feelings of others and it is important we realise this. Of course if we intentionally desire to hurt another then this another story – how do we know? Intuitively, we always know but we can also use guilt as a factor that we have not intended this situation. Each person controls their own state of being, be it a state of happiness or suffering. Those who are immersed in self-pity more of than not have the innate behaviour of making those around them feel guilty – this is a way of drawing power/love. It is very easy for sensitive people to take responsibility for others' feelings and feel guilty when they try to live their own lives for fear of hurting those who depend on them. However, it does more harm to remain in this state. For one, you inform the other person that you control their happiness and that they are incapable of doing this themselves. Secondly, you refrain from following you own truth, living your life – creating pain within yourself. Release!

Boundaries

When we take a look at our bodies, we see that we are surrounded by a boundary – our skin. This boundary has multiple purposes – protection against harmful external objects, atmospheres, friction as well as forming an exterior and definition to our inner organisms. Our skin is essentially the part of us that defines us, literally – revealing the shape of who we are and maintaining who we are to others.

Boundaries in terms of psychology and spirituality are just as important. When we relate to others, we are relating on many levels – energetically, conversationally, subconsciously – the list goes on. However, if we have not maintained our sense of boundary then we can get ourselves in to all kinds of trouble.

Issues surrounding boundaries affect both those who are more internally orientated (introverted) as well as those who are more external orientated (extroverted). An introvert responds to their internal environment in order to process their own feelings. An extrovert responds to their external environment in order to process their own feelings.

For the more sensitive amongst us, we find it difficult to maintain boundaries because our nature is used to permeating our surroundings. We live by experiencing the energies of those around us and interpret them through our own filters. As a result, sensitive people find it difficult to establish boundaries because they are so sensitive! This is because they are so sensitive to how others feel around them, that they often feel that they may hurt another's' feelings if they did anything to establish their own power. Of course, the paradox here is that sensitive people end up resenting those who they have allowed to walk over them – and no one learns anything here!

For those of us who are more internally oriented, extroverted, there is a tendency to not be aware of where our boundaries push into others. This is very common amongst those with extrovert personalities not being aware of how their personality may be infringing upon another's.

So how do we establish boundaries and what do boundaries actually mean?

Boundaries are essential in establishing who we are to others. If we do not maintain our boundaries we fall into patterns where we allow others to affect us in various negative ways. Let us look at one way in which boundaries are abused.

THE NICE TRAP

This is a common trap amongst sensitive people. When we feel we should act nice all the time to others to the extent that we are giving away substantial amounts of our own energy. Then we wonder why we have little confidence, get easily drained in explosive situations or indeed continually manifest power-victim situations! Unconditional Love is not about letting people walk all over you – it is about being True to yourself and to others in a lovingly allowing way. It is about following the truest, deepest yearning of your heart, which will naturally be aligned with the highest intentions of all. Unconditional love is about boundaries.

If you disagree with another's opinion, speak out! If you are angry with another for something they have done, express yourself! To deny your feelings is to deny the GOD within. When we keep quiet, we are not doing ourselves or the other person any favours. You might feel like you are hurting the feelings of another by telling them that they are being rude or obnoxious but if you fail to do so you are not being true to that person at all – because you are hiding what you are truly feeling. Remember their behaviour is just a cry out for help (love). By keeping it to yourself you are not fully expressing your own Being – thus giving away your power to that person, which is what they wanted in the first place! When we are being too nice to someone, we are crying out for that person to love us in return – and thus we are seeking external validation. Personal power is all about owning that which you already have.

Another problem with being nice to others (or giving too much) is the resulting resentment that occurs afterwards. When we give away too much of ourselves in an effort to please others, then sooner or later we will eventually build up enough resentment to cause ourselves grief as well as displeasure towards this other. For example, let us say that you agree to meet a friend once a week to talk about their problems. At first you feel quite good about this, thinking that you are helping them – however you have not first checked to see whether you yourself is ok with this! As the weeks pass, you already notice feelings within yourself that you would rather not. You put aside these feelings and make the agreement, feeling that it is 'better' to be nice and help your friend out. However, you have of course left out the feelings of the most important person in your life – yourself! By doing so, you may at first be able to deal with these feelings of displeasure, however sooner or later your feelings will build up to cause resentment towards this friend for taking up your time and annoying you as well as resentment towards yourself for not having stood up for yourself and making yourself clearer from the beginning.

Many of us give too much believing it to be spiritual or 'nice' or listen to others' problems. In order to check whether someone has crossed our boundaries is whether feel any animosity towards this individual. If so, we know that there is a problem to be addressed and healed.

BEING OVERTLY SELF-CONSCIOUS

Boundaries also work in terms of taking on others' energy too much and to include it into our own.

Remember, that whatever we program into our subconscious mind will manifest as the reality before us. One belief system to be thrown out is the belief that we are being constantly analysed by others. In reality we all know that it is only us that analyses ourselves to such a degree. We all assume that others are analysing us the same way we analyse/judge ourselves. There is a saying: "If you treated your friends as you treated yourself, would you have any friends?" This is because we all treat ourselves in horrific ways – always judging, criticising, analysing, condemning, comparing. The truth is that we are really concerned about ourselves and how we are perceived by others rather than the other way round – it is so easy to forget this crucial point. Our

Ego tells us that people are analysing us all the time but if this is the case then are you constantly analysing your friends?! Of course not, you wouldn't have time to live if you were assessing them and yourself 24 hours a day. The fact is that each person is more often than not focused on their own fears and desires, loves and wants. Yet the fascinating thing is that many of us very easily forget this fact.

When we are overtly self-conscious, we are acting out of a fear of being accepted. Break free of this limitation by constantly re-inventing yourself. When you are older and look back on your life, it will only be you that assesses what you have done! Have you been true to yourself or have you been fearful of what other's may think of your actions? Others won't be judging what you did 40 years ago! They will be busy with their own lives. Do you not want to look back and think, "I expressed myself as much as I could?"

Many feel like they are invading others' lives when they speak of their own lives or express a different Truth to another. This is born out of a fear of self-acceptance. When you speak your Truth, and listen to others speaking their Truths you are embarking on the most important journey that the Creator has given you. You are co-creating. And by doing this you are accelerating the spiritual growth of the whole of humanity.

FOUNTAIN VS SHIELDING & PROTECTION

There are many techniques being taught on how to protect oneself against negativity – other people's negativity and against psychic attacks. Whilst it is very important to maintain integrity within one's auric field, the word protection and what it implies still resides with our subconscious mind. Protection implies that one is under attack – that one needs to protect oneself because one is powerless to do so otherwise. The subconscious can only interpret this in one way – that others are out to get you, watch out! And also that you are too weak as your own being and you need a shield.

What must be recognised is that there is no one out to get you and there is no one who can make you feel anything. The Laws of Free Will, Attraction and Reflection mean that we only attract into our energies that which we already resonate. Negativity that we draw from others will be attracted to negativity that lies within ourselves. *Unless* we are strong enough within our own Light that this negativity will not even affect us. And herein lies the solution.

Instead of seeing the world and your friends and those on the train or passers-by as your enemy, which protection inevitably teaches, see them as your long-lost brothers and sisters – for that in reality is who they are. If you feel 'under attack' from negativity from others, then first notice that it is you that is pulling this energy in. So stop. Turn your consciousness inward and recognise that it is only your perception that is allowing their negativity to merge with your own. Begin to see yourself as a powerful dynamo of love light and begin to flood your energy out like a fountain. This love, as white light will then transform their energy and help them as well. As we can see simply protection against other people's negativity doesn't actually help anyone – all it does is reiterate the belief that we need a shield, that we are under attack (a victim) and that others are an enemy. Flooding your Light out and shining for others has a very different effect – it will empower you as a powerful being, help transform the individual you are encountering and spread the message of Love and Inclusion as opposed to fear and separation.

What is important is to maintain our integrity. To empower ourselves and work on ourselves and fill ourselves with self-love so that this love can then shine and flood out to others to help them transform. Maintaining integrity means that you look after yourself, you take care of your physical body and energetic body. Practice regular chakra cleanses to clean out your own energy field then this will help when with others of course! Always remember the law of attraction – what resonates with us will be attracted. So you want to attract light, loving, joyful, passionate people? Then resonate this within yourself! If you are not reflecting that, that is not a bad thing – simply more experience for your experiences.

Sympathy

Sympathy can have the undesired effect of causing more harm than good. When another comes to you for help and feels sorry for themselves – be wary of falling into the trap of empowering their belief by giving them your energy of sympathy. This helps neither them or you, for you are losing energy by being sympathetic whilst continuing to empower their belief that they are a victim. Lovingly tell them they are strong. Tenderly tell them to shrug off their feelings of bitterness for it serves no one any good to be bitter. Use compassion to show them the real gifts of their pain and they will be able to see why they have been trapped by these vicious cycles for so long. Feelings of unworthiness and victimisation only cloud a person's perception of the world and makes them slaves to their Ego. Gently tell them to see with their eyes open – life is truly abundant if we stop getting caught in vicious cycles of self-victimisation and self-sympathy. If you find you encounter people who talk negatively all the time about things, change the nature of the conversation to bring light into it, for fear cannot challenge the might of Light. Soon their spirit will be unable to resist the lure of your loving nature and they will learn to ignore the lure of their dominant fear-based Ego.

It is important to use compassion instead of sympathy. Sympathy labels others as victims, where they are powerless against an outside force. Compassion sees the power in all – in both the 'victim' and yourself – bringing responsibility back to that other who may be suffering, allowing them the power to then escape it. No one really needs anyone else's saving, what they may need however is support and guidance and ultimately love. Compassion is the key as it leads to helping both that person in front of you in a real way and yourself by not giving away your energy, just Love.

SELFISHNESS VS. SELFLESSNESS

Loving someone does not mean making their feelings more important than your own. Love is a two-way process.

When we love ourselves and follow our own Truth, we act like a beacon for others to follow in our footsteps. By acting as an example, others want to learn your secret and this is one of the most effective ways of helping people. Let go of the old conditioning that being true to your-Self is being selfish – this is simply *un*true. Being untrue to yourself is the cause of all problems. Ensure you are following your highest truth and this will *always* allow and honour the highest truth of others.

Some may attack you for following your own path at first but remember this is a test of your resolve. You know deep down if you are being selfish and whether the another is trapped in a power game, needing you to be locked in misery like they are. For this makes them feel more secure. People become fearful when others break free of the mass sheep consciousness.

How do we know when to be selfish and when to be selfless? We always know when to be selfless because it will feel good within us. If being selfless is born from guilt or because we feel we "have to" then we know that we are not really being selfless and that this is another form of a power game.

When we serve others, we are also serving ourselves. This is not a selfish concept, for our relationship to others depends upon our relationship to ourselves. An individual who has no inward perception and believes they are serving others selflessly often helps through sympathy - however sympathy serves no-one! Sympathy asks for appreciation and gratuity in return and claims another is a victim just like the one offering the sympathy. Compassion recognises the strength of all, including those that are suffering. Also remember that when we give to others, we receive in many ways - including learning from those we are assisting - we each have something to learn from another. So we move away from being someone's saviour to being someone's guide, as they guide us and teach us about their life. When we realise this truth, we allow ourselves to recognise that in reality there is no such thing as selfless service, for all service serves also the Self! Respect and serve yourself, only then can only respect and serve others.

Avoid the martyr syndrome. Know that others are going through pain for a reason, they have chosen it, they have created it, for some reason or another. You can help them as much as you can but understand people's reasons for doing things for these choices are all born out of their free will. They wish to grow just as you do. They may try to draw you in but know that you can help in your own special way, through compassion.

We now live in a world where there are masses upon masses of *Lightworkers* following their own truth so do not be afraid. Once you make that first step, you will be rewarded by attracting all those free spirits like you. You are the way showers – you are the warriors. Much will be given to you because much will be expected. Be Strong and you will be rewarded.

CREATING YOUR SACRED SPACE

LOOKING AFTER YOUR HUMAN VESSEL

Your human body is a magnificent temple, housing your magnificent Spirit. As spiritual beings in physical form, we are able to utilise the physical body to help regulate our state of being. Naturally our state of being will be reflected in our body.

The physical body represents an extension of our Spirit, it is a beautiful anchor on this realm, where we can experience physicality. Therefore we must endeavour to treat our human body with the love and care that it deserves, for it is an extension of our Divine Self.

EXERCISE

This helps regulate the flow of energy throughout your system. As the cardiovascular system is pumped up, the flow of blood around the body helps the flow of energy and our chakras begin to release blockages within us. Remember you are a spiritual being inhabiting a *physical* body. You are here to balance mind, *body* and spirit – so endeavour to exercise well and keep your body healthy for otherwise it will affect you in all areas of your life. Each of the mind, body and spirit are interconnected to each other in various ways – what happens to one will affect the other two

WATER

Drink plenty of water. Water is the essence of life on the physical plane. It purifies the body, mind and soul and releases toxins from the body, which can build up to cause an array of problems. It is also the metaphoric representation of your emotions.

HEALTH: PHYSICAL AILMENTS AND DISEASES

When we suffer physical ailments in our lives it is a direct reflection of our state of being. Our thoughts pass from our subconscious mind through the levels of energy until they reach our body, where they manifest into physical reality. When we feel anxiety in our consciousness then this stress can be reflected in our human vessel.

Stress, by its very nature, condenses and suppresses energy. When we feel stress, we literally block the flow of energy within our entire system. Since the physical vessel relies on the energy that flows through it and keeps it regulated, blockages such as this can cause us serious harm if we allow it to build up.

Disease reflects a dis-ease within our consciousness. When we are stressed, we allow for the influx of negativity to contaminate our energetic system. Remember, the human vessel is simply the densest part of the auric field. Our body, physical matter, is simply energy moving at a very slow speed. So, if we allow negativity, a very dense vibration to flood our field, we bring our entire system down. From another point of view, our stress creates blockages within our energy flow, which then coagulates to cause us pain.

The physical body acts as a library of information for the state of our consciousness. Just as those around us are a reflection of the state of our consciousness, so is our human vessel. To target the cause of disease, we literally move our awareness to the cause. Where did this physical ailment arise from? *When* did it arise?

When we look for the *cause* within our consciousness, we see the reasons behind the *effect* in our physical body. Of course, this is not to discount medical science or forms of energetic healing, for these provide us with time to deal with the cause. However, in all cases, it is not a drug or a healing session that heals you. It is *you* that heals you. For *only you can heal you!*

When you want to be healed and target the cause of that healing with your awareness, either consciously or superconsciously, then you begin the process of healing. By loving your-Self and respecting your physical vessel, you allow your entire being to vibrate in harmony with *All That Is*. Here there is no dis-ease, for there is only infinite ease and grace.

CONNECTING WITH NATURE & GROUNDING

Grounding is essential because so much of the spiritual experience seems to suggest we look upwards to connect. Of course, we look inwards to connect! However, the above and below serve as our greater connection the Universal existence. The above represents the father, whilst the below represents the mother. Gaia, the Earth, nourishes us and gives us life. The Earth provides us with everything we need to survive. It is our connection with Mother Earth that represents our umbilical cord, replenishing, feeding and nurturing us.

Nature allows us to connect with Gaia, Mother Earth, to establish the connection with the physical world. The high vibrational frequency among plants, trees and open space cleanse our bodies in a multitude of ways.

Feel the air as the breath of GOD. See the gentle movement of the leaves and trees as the expression of Gaia. Feel the sun's beam infiltrating every part of your being, purifying and cleansing and revitalising your very essence. It is the Love Light of Source that you see before you. Bask in all its glory, it is there for you to receive.

You can connect with the Earth simply by spending time in nature. We so often tell ourselves that we don't have time to relax in nature or walk in nature, but we do! And deep down we know we have at least half an hour a week to walk in nature. Just walking in a park or sitting by a tree can revitalise and reconnect our energy systems with the Earth. Our vibrational frequencies then align with that of the Earth, which is where we spend all our waking time! If we are out of sync with the Earth, our energies become dissipated – we are ungrounded. And this can affect everything in our lives, from the way we respond to energy (other people's energy) to the way we feel internally. Remember, the Earth is a part of us, as we a part of her.

"The frog does not drink up the pond in which he lives"
Sioux, Native American proverb

Respecting the Earth is to respect ourselves. The Earth nourishes us with everything we need – the air, food, water, shelter. The Earth is literally our Mother, fulfilling our needs. If we do not respect the Earth, we are only destroying our own habitat. We have for a very long time disregarded the importance of our reliance upon the Earth. More importantly we have misunderstood our integral connection with Gaia.

Gaia is a complex bubble of biology. Just as we are bubbles of biology walking around on the planet, our bubbles interact and integrate with other bubbles of biology around us. For example, the plants emit oxygen, which we breathe. We breathe out carbon dioxide, which *they* breathe! Everything relies upon the existence of another and to take one out, we threaten the whole eco-system – the whole planet.

Do we disrespect our own mothers, after all they have done for us? They have fed us, clothed us, nurtured us…they have given birth to us! Mother Earth has also given birth to all of us, allowing us to reside on her beautiful surface, allowing us to interact with her offspring – the plants, the trees, the oceans.

We must endeavour to begin using our awareness more and more in our realities. Just because something seems inanimate or 'just alive', does not necessarily mean it is so. Everything is intricately connected. Your bubble of biology is interacting with every single bubble of biology on this planet, including the people, the trees, the animals and ultimately the Earth as a whole. With each and every one of us respecting and looking after Mother Earth, we allow ourselves as children to play and benefit from this beautiful planet. Similarly, our children and their children will benefit from this also. Isn't this what we want?

The Earth is a paradise, it is *already* the Garden of Eden. It is simply up to us to treat it that way. Instead of working against the planet, it is up to each of us to work with the planet. Instead of making the planet accommodate us, let us think for a moment and realise which came first? Which is providing unconditional support and nourishment to the other? So, instead of working against the planet, it is more rational and more evolved to work *with* the planet.

The more our awareness grows, the more we realise just how everything is interconnected with one another and we begin to see the effects of every single decision we make in life. This truth includes how we treat the Earth. It is not simply a place that exists for our use and abuse. The Earth is a conscious living organism, on a *grand* scale. By disrespecting the Earth, we are really disrespecting ourselves, since everything is connected. We are all ONE.

All change begins at home, with each of us. By making each step, no matter how small, makes all the difference in the end.

Also remember that you have your own personal connection to Gaia that is completely unique. This is not a new connection, for you have been here before, countless times. Every time you incarnate, you say hello to your most-dearly beloved sister and mother. Say hello again and remember your Divine and eternal connection to one of the most beautiful beings in existence – Planet Earth.

LISTENING TO YOUR INTUITION

"Our first teacher is our own heart"
Cheyenne proverb

Your inner voice knows ALL. We all have intuition. It is how we react to or respond to our intuition that defines our connection to Spirit.

Spirit is constantly whispering to you. Your Inner Spirit (Infinite Self) is your eternal guide, nudging you this way and that so that you may be happy. When you are still, when you quieten the mind of all the chaos that distracts it, then you provide a space for Spirit's whisperings to become louder and clearer. This is because the Higher realms work on higher vibrational frequencies. On the Earth plane, we are functioning at a very low frequency. To connect to our Higher Selves and spiritual guides, we raise our vibrational frequency to match that of the upper realms and this is done through meditation or deep relaxation. Our Higher Selves will also endeavour to lower their frequencies as well to help match ours, however because of free will you have to do the hard work here! Soon however it will become second nature for you to bring your-Self into a state of deep relaxation and interconnectedness. As with everything, it takes practice!

Intuition is that guiding voice that knows everything about you. Your Infinite Self knows all of your past lives, all of your potential futures, all of your feelings, all of your pain, all of your joy, all of your wants and of your needs. It has no judgement just unwavering devotion to You. The intuition that you hear whispering to you is always trying to protect and inspire you, but never infringing on your free will.

Your inner voice speaks through Love, it knows your Highest Truth and will endeavour to help you in every way possible. It will playfully guide you through your life, always looking for new ways in which you can experience happiness and joy whilst learning your life lessons. Other ways of accessing the wisdom of Spirit is through writing or channelling, which again involves various forms of meditation. Writing is simply a channelled form of meditation, where the mind is forced to focus on one area. Your inner voice will sound as if it is your own thoughts at first. This is because *it is* you! Imagination is often thought to be that which is made up. Yet imagination is the source of your intuition! Refrain from dismissing what you perceive as imagination when you begin to seek your Inner Voice, for it is through your imagination that you are being spoken to.

Write a journal of answers that you receive when you ask questions to your Inner Spirit. At first you may feel that you are making it all up and that is in your imagination. Yet your intuition is speaking through to you more clearly than you think. After a few weeks, you may see a pattern and perceive an undulation of messages speaking through your suggested imagination.

Imagination is the source and arena of your playground. As you ask questions, you may at first dismiss many of the answers because you say to yourself, "I just imagined that". Yes you did imagine that but trust what you imagined! For example, you may use the traffic light form of asking your Inner Spirit questions. Here, centre yourself and then ask your Infinite Self, GOD, the Universe, your guides, or whomever you desire a question that requires a yes or no answer. Then immediately picture a traffic light and see what colour that traffic light is revealing itself as to you. Is it Red? Is it Green? Is it Amber? Take the first thing that comes to your mind. And this is the true nature of learning to access Spirit. The first thing that comes to your mind is untainted by your own filters. We often call the first thing that comes to our mind our imagination but in reality that is the source of your intuition.

Remember, your Inner Spirit is just as desperate to make contact with you as you are with it. You both form the Union that is One as you are both incomplete without the other.

Being Still / Meditation

Taking time to yourself each day is vital to your well-being. Time to detach yourself from emotions and to shrug off others' conditioning, opinions, negativity and movies. Realise the gift that you are living, that you exist. Sometimes for many of us it takes a life-threatening accident to realise how precious life is and how we worry about such inconsequential things. You do not need to experience such suffering, be still in this very moment and see the wonder of existence that is Yours to claim.

In this very moment, as you read these words, connect to each and every other reader that also reads these words. Time is irrelevant. This holy instant is all that exists. You are forever connected with each other, the entire Universe, and all of existence, past, present and future. This sacred moment will last forever and can be accessed whenever. This is a very powerful realisation. We are all continuously connected through the Power of NOW. There is only NOW. We can connect to any part of our-Self and another at any time through the magic of our consciousness. You can BE at this moment whenever you want. This moment always exists, don't you see? At this moment, we are ONE.

Why do we want to be still? Because when we are still we are in the knowing of who we are. When you still the mind you see beyond the illusion of fear and you return to the Truth that "I AM". I AM consciousness. You are the essence of everything. Silence isn't silent! Silence is the infinite arena of Being. When you experience silence and are observing life, in nature for example, you are truly seeing. You have switched off the turbulent chattering of the mind and have come to a place where dreams are manifest and creations are born. It is here where our power lies. This infinite arena of potentiality.

When you are still, you connect deeply with everything and from this space you have access to infinite knowledge, infinite creativity and infinite possibilities. From this space, you are also able to grasp the eternal Truth – that You are Perfection in Bliss.

When you are still, you are open to creating space for ideas to be born. Inspiration and creativity are born within this stillness of the spirit – for it is here where you align yourselves to the very essence of your being.

Make a pledge to yourself to constantly be on guard of your thoughts and to give yourself time and love *daily* – thus allowing you to BE-come all that you are all the more quickly. It need not take more than half an hour in our day or even five minutes.

SECTION FOUR
INFINITE BEING
LIVING THE LAW OF REFLECTION

The Law of Reflection
New Paradigm Law of Attraction

We are now entering a new frequency of being. With this comes newer ways of perceiving reality. We are moving from a dualistic state (good, bad, right, wrong) into a nondualistic state (oneness, nonjudgement, being).

The Law of Attraction has taught us well. It shows us that we can Create. This is its ultimate purpose. However it is important we recognise why this has come into our Global Consciousness. We are moving from a "want" society into a "being" society. Our current society, and that preceding it, has been founded upon wanting. There are many reasons for this of course and this is partly due to our inherent human belief that we are separate. When we believe we are separate we believe that love (power) needs to be externally sourced.

The Law of Attraction in its current state asks us what we want. What do you want? What you want, you will create and attract.

However, let us ask one very important question. Why are you here? Why are you here on this planet?

For many people, the Law of Attraction (with its current mainstream understanding) does not work and there is a reason for this. The Law of Attraction is here to show us that Yes, We Create Our Reality. You are a Creator. However, it is important to remember something. You have been creating since the moment you entered this planet. How were you doing that unconsciously?

The Law of Reflection

As we look deeper we see that there is something else, also linked to the Law of Attraction that may help us understand our state of reality and being on a deeper level.

Your external reality is a mirror of your internal consciousness. Everything around you is a direct reflection of Who You Are. The emotions you radiate out into the Universe work to vibrationally match with those around, and using the Law of Attraction, bring this into your space.

Why would this be? One of the most beautiful aspects of this reality is that when we see what is occurring externally, we understand the being within. We understand who we are by literally experiencing who we are!

There are several factors we need to recognise here:

We do not know what we want to Create. Currently using the Law of Attraction, we are assumed to know what we want to create. We are asked to put out what we want. Do we really know what we want? The majority of our wants are passed through our Egos, based on our conditionings, our experiences and of course the feelings we have towards ourselves (the level of our self-love). So the idea that we can know what we want is always shown to us when we move through different cycles and become more of who we are - naturally what we want has changed!

Recognising that we do not know what want allows us to surrender to the Greater Order that surrounds and permeates us. You are an integral part of this Greater Order. You are All That Is.

There are THREE other Creators involved in your Creation process

You are not the only one Creating. We are moving from a Singular perspective of reality towards a Oneness perspective. The singular perspective has been vital however in allowing us to understand our personal power. It is time for us to recognise our part in the Greater Picture.

There are three parties involved in your Creations:

- You (the Creator)
- Humanity (your Co-Creators)
- The Universe (the unseen guiding force)

Whenever you radiate your emotions into the Universe, you are being matched to the vibration of others that match you. However, what you may be may not coincide with what others are being in your space. Therefore, the Universe will ensure that the match is made perfectly.

The Universe is also involved in your Creations. This effectively means Your Higher Self (or Greater Infinite Self who knows all). Imagine if you will a tall building in a city. You are on the ground floor. This is your Conscious human Self. Your Higher Self is in the Penthouse of this building. From your perspective on the ground, you can see around you laterally, the roads going off in front, behind, left and right. You make choices and decisions for yourself based on your free will. You take a road to the left or right, in front or behind. This is your Path.

Your Higher Self however sees all. It can see beyond the horizon. It can see where these paths may take you. Try as you might you may desire to force yourself down a road which looks flowery and bloomy from your perspective. However your Higher Self may see from the perspective of the penthouse that this road may weave around into a ditch! Your higher Self knows what is best for you. Remember your Higher Self is You, it only seems separate within this reality, separated by the veil of illusion, separating your Consciousness. That veil is also breaking down as you become more and more attuned to what your Higher Self is vibrating out to you.

What does this mean? It means that we may be trying to Create a reality that does not serve us, because we are doing it from a place of our wants/desires. How do we know what is our wants/desires and not? The truth is when we are feeling something, we don't know where it is coming from and we are less than willing to listen sometimes not to go down a path that may not effectively serve us. However, this doesn't matter as we are feeling that emotion for a reason and it is important we feel everything. There is no wrong and there is no wrong path. It is all part of our Path.

ACTIVE vs PASSIVE

One of the aspects of the Law of Attraction is that it gives the impression that everything comes to us. This formulates a belief system within our consciousness that we are in a waiting mode. I will have that career when it comes to me. I will meet my partner when they come to me. I will have this money when it comes to me.

Life is for Living. When we are waiting, we are not anchoring our Spirit into this realm and we are not truly Living. Your Spirit wants to explore. It is by nature an Explorer. It wants to discover more about itself. Break boundaries that it feels limited by, personality-wise, culturally, societally. When we open ourselves up and create and explore opportunities, open doors and take the initiative, we start a phenomenal process. We are moving energy. We are declaring to the Universe that we are loving life, this in return attracts a similar vibration.

Being active allows us to explore life. We are not supposed to know all of the answers, of what is going to happen to us, when, how, where, why. We are here to live, and to create the life we want. Literally. Whatever it is you desire, take the initiative. This not only opens more doors for your desire to be brought to you, it simultaneously opens your personality for tremendous growth. And this is what your Spirit wants. It wants to grow, to be freed from limitation.

Break out of your box. Whatever box that may be. Speak to 'strangers', apply for work, explore. In spiritual circles we can tell ourselves that it "doesn't feel right" so I won't go down there. However, we do not know that by opening a door, something that does feel right may appear! There is nothing to lose, ever, by exploring a path. If it truly does not resonate then we already know it doesn't serve us. However, if it is more procrastination about our life and waiting for something, then we also know we are the ones who aren't moving, not our reality!

We are here on a physical realm to live physically. That is the beauty of this place. Opportunities are around everywhere, and with that comes synchronicity. The more we step forward, the more the Universe responds and opens up. Our life becomes limitless. Possibilities limitless. Happiness limitless.

Purpose & Meaning
The Divine Plan

Destiny

The choices you make, the path you lead, the people you meet are all entwined within your Destiny. There is nothing you can do wrong, or do badly or be in any way "off your path". It is all your Destiny.

Our Destiny leads us where we are meant to be. The emotions you feel, the so-called setbacks you have are all planned specifically with higher wisdom that you experience them! It is all part of your Destiny.

With this in mind, what we want to create will be in harmony with our Destiny. So the key thing to think about here is Why are we trying to control what we want to create?

The Law of Attraction when looked at in its current form does not take into account higher reasoning, essentially here, global consciousness and its purpose. You have a purpose here and this is why you are here. What you may be trying to Create for yourself may not be harmony with the Divine Plan for humanity.

We are taught that when we are not able to create something there must be something wrong with us. Maybe we have a fear of money? Maybe we have a fear of commitment? Maybe we have a fear of creating?! This is a polarised (and judgemental) way of looking at ourselves. You are experiencing exactly what you are meant to be experiencing, for a reason. Whatever you are going through is because it is a reflection of your inner journey, and this is Perfect. We are meant to be experiencing what we are, for reasons beyond our current understanding and once we let go and surrender to that, we realise that there is nothing wrong with what we are doing, we are simply being and flowing with what is occurring.

When we fight our reality, we are fighting ourselves. For we are the ones who have created it! When we judge our reality and judge what we can or cannot create, we are also judging ourselves. For we do not appreciate the depth of what is being given to us. Greater Experience. Whatever current situation you may be in, has been gifted to you. It is a gift, because there is something very deep, golden and precious for you to emerge victorious with during and following that experience. That golden wisdom will catapult you spiritually into higher realms of being. This Spiritual Growth effectively brings you greater happiness, wisdom and the ability to share and express to those around you, who could benefit from your experience.

Let us take an example and look at the current difficulty in creating money by many, to survive. Traditionally we are being taught that this is because we have fears of abundance and worthiness of receiving it. However, this is still a polarised way of looking at what is occurring. There is nothing wrong with you. You are who you are. So why would so many be experiencing something simultaneously? it's important we ask the questions and look collectively as it may hold the answers to what is happening internally. What if there is something happening collectively related to entire concept of money? These are the times of the Ascension and Paradigm Shift, where everything is shifting - because humanity is shifting. We cannot understand what has been planned. However, we can look at our own lives and see that maybe it is asking something else of us. Maybe to source our security within ourselves, as opposed to within the concept of money. Yes this is very difficult, however we are being asked to trust in the unseen. To trust in ourselves.

When we stand in our truth and power, what will happen? That is what we are being asked. It is always up to us to discover and locate the ultimate wisdom within any situation and take it, for our own.

LIVING THE MAGIC WITH THE LAW OF REFLECTION

Living the Law of Reflection requires us now to understand our place in the Universe. Yes, we are each able to create our own reality. Yet we are also creating our reality in conjunction with the creations of all other beings in existence. This includes all others on our plane and those who are guiding us, as well as of course the higher will of the entire Universe.

Whilst we are in control, we are also not. This is the paradox of life. When we submit our will to the Universe, we are in alignment with all that exists. For the Universe is a part of you. When you submit to the greater cause, you are allowing the unknown to become a true force in your life. It is here where the miracles occur, where life becomes the mysterious playground that is joyful to live in!

If we are telling ourselves that we must use intention in order to create then surely we will all be sitting at home repeating affirmations in order to create! What kind of life would that be?

When we are living in harmony with the Universe, we are not using affirmations or visualisations at all! We are simply living in joy and within that, comes the experience of a child. This allows true magic to occur as we move through life in wonderful surprise, amazement and joy at the events that are being brought towards us.

This as you will notice is a very different way of living than where we are creating outwards. For in this second scenario we are appreciating and in a state of wonder at everything that is given to us, thanking the Universe for mysteriously and synchronistically bringing everything to us.

You are living in Magic. You are the Magic. Surrender to the Universe. Surrender to Yourself.

Synchronicity, Living the Magic, Community

Living the Law of Reflection requires us now to understand our place in the Universe. Yes, we are each able to create our own reality. Yet we are also creating our reality in conjunction with the creations of all other beings in existence. This includes all others on our plane and those who are guiding us, as well as of course the higher will of the entire Universe.

Whilst we are in control, we are also not. This is the paradox of life. When we submit our will to the Universe, as the wonderful Sufis teach us so eloquently, we are in alignment with All That Is. For the Universe is a part of you. When you submit to the greater cause, you are allowing the unknown to become a true force in your life. It is here where the miracles occur, where life becomes the mysterious playground that is joyful to live in!

If we are telling ourselves that we must use intention in order to create then surely we will all be sitting at home repeating affirmations in order to create! What kind of life would that be?

When we are living in harmony with the Universe, we are not using affirmations or visualisations at all! We are simply living in joy and within that, comes the experience of a child. This allows true magic to occur as we move through life in wonderful surprise, amazement and joy at the events that are being brought towards us.

This as you will notice is a very different way of living than where we are creating outwards. For in this second scenario we are appreciating and in a state of wonder at everything that is given to us, thanking the Universe for mysteriously and synchronistically bringing everything to us.

Being (Conscious Creative Playing) = *Living* Your Reality

This is the most crucial aspect of creating your reality. Balancing the spiritual and the material, the receptive and the active. When you draw from Spirit, you must be able to apply it in physical reality. In other words, when you manifest you must be able to then live that reality.

To get to this point of course, we need to have a good grasp of our own Self, and this is the constant awareness of our own energies and issues, hence why the majority of this book has been directed at who we are. For when we are in a continual exploration of who we are, we recognise that life is a reflection of us. Our immediate awareness of our own reality ignites the chain reaction that then heals and transforms it into powerful aspects, thus changing our reality further.

Our higher consciousness, or higher Self, can be seen in some ways as working literally from a higher level. If we think of ourselves in a multi-story building, we can see our conscious Self on the ground floor, enjoying life (we should hope!) on the Earth plane. Our higher Self is at the top floor, observing reality. It is from this vantage point, from this perspective that the higher Self can see more of the ground level. The conscious Self can only see as far as its own horizon, which is limited from the ground level. Not to mention the many other buildings and paths and challenges that surround. The higher Self can see over these challenges, what lies beyond. The higher Self can see all paths. Yet the higher Self recognises that the conscious Self needs to move through these parts.

Of course you are both the conscious Self AND the higher Self simultaneously. You are the building! This is the Greater Self. You are simply raising your awareness between your levels of consciousness. The "higher Self" has awareness in infinite space – so this infinite wisdom simply cannot exist in its totality in finite space (Earth reality). And this is beautiful, for in finite reality we surrender to the greater unknown, the infinite, to recognise our place in this reality, in the Universe.

What is happening in your life that you feel is causing you stress *in this moment*? There is no doubt that you are stressed or feeling anxiety because this issue, you cannot deny your feelings because you are feeling them! Instead, accept that you are feeling those feelings and then ask yourself, what would my higher aspect be seeing right now? And you can raise your awareness to this level of being. To the top floor of the building and see out into your reality. See with your heart. Why would you be experiencing what you are experiencing? Take in as much wisdom as you can – from yourself. We are never given all the answers for this is where the unknown comes in. We take our confidence of knowing there are paths ahead of us, many roads through the City, simply because we have faith. It is faith that takes us to a place of unparalleled freedom, where we are in total surrender to All That Is. We have faith in us and we have faith in where we will be. This allows us to *flow!*

We all hear this saying "Live in the NOW" but do we really understand its purpose and meaning?

When we live in the present moment, we align ourselves with our True infinite Self, for this is where Spirit resides. The NOW is the reality of eternal existence. Time is an illusory concept that we have designed to better our evolution on this plane. However, in reality the past, present and future are all simultaneous.

Consciousness is eternal and represents the timeless existence that is *All That Is*. We are consciousness, journeying through the various wonders of creation that you have set out to further our knowledge of all things. When we centre our consciousness onto the present moment, we are letting go of all our attachments to the past and future and this is an extremely powerful process. For when our consciousness remains in the past or in a future event then we are misaligned with our Spirit. We are focusing on something that has already occurred or something that has yet to occur, ignoring the fact that existence resides in the present moment.

When we focus on a past event, we are blinding ourselves to our creative powers. For as we focus our attention on the past, we are constantly changing the past to whatever suits our emotions or adapting and manipulating it in our minds to make us feel better or worse. This will ultimately affect present and future events because we are *always* creating. Living in the future, means that we are focusing on events that are yet to be and are shifting our creative powers again away from the present moment and are placing our energy in events that have not occurred. In reality, the past is not set in stone as we have been so long led to believe.

The past is just as malleable as the present and future. Past events can be manipulated in our minds to anything that we desire. Let us take a simple example: a woman has memories of being betrayed by a partner quite early on in her teenage years. Throughout her life, this woman has been at the whim of her insecurities of being betrayed. This feeling and resulting deep well of emotions have caused this woman a number of problems in securing positive relationships with men.

Now let us meet this woman at an important time in her later life, one where she chosen to deal with her fears and insecurities of being betrayed. As the woman heals the pains within herself, she begins to transmute the past event into something completely different. Instead the deep insecurity becomes one of the woman's greatest strengths as she transmutes it into wisdom. She chooses not to remain stuck in self-pity, remorse and self-hate and instead learns to love her-Self. She learns to see that it is her that allows another to hurt her and so she chooses not to take his power from others but to draw it from within. This bears a confidence in her that she has never had and resultantly boosts her relating with men. So here we can see that the past event has in fact changed, for this woman no longer views it as painful but now sees it as something far grander, something that has actually made her more confident than she would have ever been.

The point here is that the same memory has at least two versions. The past is malleable. We can see that the betrayal is both devastatingly painful as well as something extraordinarily magical.

When we get locked in past events, we become sucked into the past (a place that does not really exist). The past is only what we see it for in our minds. It is constantly changing, depending on our moods, and state of being. When we are depressed, we pick out all the things in our life where we have been wronged or where we have suffered. When we are happy, we look back and we see all the events in our life that have led to this moment of happiness – we see a chain of events that have led to this moment and we pick out the events that brought us joy and see our painful events as challenges not obstacles.

So we can see that we are *always* manipulating the past into whatever we desire. The point here is then to ignore the callings of the Ego to pick out the so-called negative things that have occurred and see only with our angel eyes – i.e. see the sufferings we have had as vital lessons that have made us stronger and see the events that brought us joy as happiness – it's *all* good.

The past is very similar to the future, in that it is malleable. We constantly worry about future events when it hasn't occurred. Or we fantasise about future events without actually living. When we centre ourselves in the present moment, we form a sacred union with our Divine Self and allow more and more of our True Self to shine forth in our Earthly lives. This allows us to regain more and more of our inherent powers as Supreme Creators of this reality.

The present moment is all that exists. The present moment is where all creations are born. It is where you are always creating. You cannot create from the past and you cannot create from the future. So when you are locked into mind dramas in the past or the future, you are denying your-Self the most precious gift of all – the gift of Creating Your Reality. Embrace this gift by embracing the eternal Truth that is existence and existence resides in the infinite that is the present moment.

True existence comes from letting go of our attachments – our attachments to the past and our attachments to our future plans. Herein lies our freedom and the freedom to embrace what life really has to offer us. Here we become alert to all the miracles that are ever present and we are able to seize the opportunities that present themselves to us. Live NOW.

Decisions, Decisions

Each moment brings us face to face with possibilities - choices, various roads we can take. Yet most of the time we have such trouble specifying a path for ourselves. Why are decisions so difficult to make?

By examining the causes of our indecisions, we are gifted with awareness. Through awareness, we achieve liberation, as we come to a place where all roads are open and perfect. We realise and accept the greatest gift of all - Free Will.

Fearing the Future

One of the main reasons for our indecisiveness is our fear of future instability - or more aptly, fear of future insecurity.

Every decision we make leads to a path. All paths are uncertain because they concern the future - and are therefore unpredictable. All uncertain and unpredictable paths are unstable. Why does being unstable cause us fear?

This is because we tell ourselves that external things, such as friends, family, lovers, situations, career and money, can make us happy. All these factors represent a pool of power that we draw from to give us happiness. Power is synonymous with love. We endeavour to seek this power, this love, externally because we do not believe we can source it from ourselves - we do not love ourselves.

As we draw power (love) from these externalities, we perpetuate our state of instability through our dependence upon them. This is because as those externalities fluctuate and change, we become disorientated and ultimately lose our power source - we become unhappy.

And this is where this philosophy of fearing uncertainty (the future) emanates from. The future is uncertain and therefore unable to offer us definite security. When we realise that our happiness is reliant upon something that is inherently unstable, we realise that drawing power externally does not serve us. As we begin to draw from within, we create the very essence of security. The more we draw security (power/love) from within, the more this security becomes something that is harmless to external influence.

This enables us to have a completely different perspective and experience of our reality. Instead of allowing external people, experiences and situations to control our choices, we allow ourselves to make the decisions. It is when we allow externalities to make our decisions that cause us such pain. This is because we know our true decisions are not being met. Would you like it if your parents made all your decisions for you? Of course not! You want to make your own decisions. Then treat all externalities in the same manner!

As we learn to believe in ourselves more and more, we open ourselves up more and more to a world of infinite possibilities.

Distrust of Ourselves

Another factor for our indecisions is that we simply do not believe in ourselves. We do not believe that we are capable of making a sound decision that will lead to a positive result. Whenever we are undecided about something, we are basically saying to ourselves "I am uncertain whether this decision I make is right. Therefore I am uncertain of my own ability to make right decisions". This is a direct reflection of how we feel internally about ourselves. If we were confident and secure about ourselves, we would not be concerned about making "wrong" decisions.

Our internal fears always emerge to inform us that we are simply incapable of making a decision that could lead to a positive experience. We doubt.

So let us ask, what is doubt? If we look at our language definition of doubt we see the words distrust, disbelief and uncertainty prop up. And this is what doubt is - it is a distrust of ourselves. Our internal and external conditioning informs us that we have no right to believe in ourselves. We dictate to ourselves that we are simply incapable of making a correct choice. When we have little belief of our own power to make correct choices then this will be reflected in our outer world. We will literally approach people, situations and experiences with this negative belief (insecurity) of not having an effective power.

DOUBT OVER OUR ABILITY TO HANDLE TOUGH EXPERIENCES

Another aspect of our distrust is our belief that we are incapable of facing certain situations. When we fear making wrong decisions, we basically fear a possible negative future event and how we may be placed in it. Ultimately, we also fear our ability to handle that possible negative situation.

If we were truly confident, secure and empowered in ourselves we would not fear any situation or experience because we would know we could handle it and not be negatively affected by it. Therefore, all roads would be open.

This point ties in with another crucial factor of where we are still seeing the world in terms of good and bad, right and wrong, black and white. This is polarity consciousness. This is the paradox of our distrust. On one hand, we do not trust our ability to make "right" decisions. On the other hand, we harbour a belief in right and wrong in the first place! However, it is important that we approach both points separately because both individually offer us respective growth as we overcome them. As we evolve our awareness to see as a compassionate being, we see the truth, beauty and splendour in all things.

All situations have an opportunity of growth as all situations serve us. To fear situations and experiences only empowers potent messages to our subconscious mind that we are weak because we are unable to handle certain situations. It is imperative for our own happiness that we do not simply label an experience as negative since this will tie us to it. When we see the Light in all situations, we move on and become happier, wiser and stronger - we grow. It is therefore crucial that we change the way we perceive all our experiences. We must endeavour to see the purpose in all things.

It is also essential that we believe in our own ability to handle any situation. There is not one situation that we cannot handle. It is only our disbelief in ourselves that causes us to shrink from pain and suffering, thus making that pain and suffering affect us more! If we really fear our ability to handle negative situations, we will literally force ourselves to live under a rock for the rest of our lives. Yet this still does not hide us from negative situations! A fearful ostrich that hides its head under the sand, still has its entire body open to attack! You simply cannot run from your fear - and this is not something to fear either! It is a part of you that you have yet to heal, embrace and transmute into a positive trait.

Where a choice leads to a so-called mistake, it has highlighted a part of you that needs healing anyway. Whether you experience that 'mistake' now or later is irrelevant, it is a part of you that must be addressed and healed if you are truly to be fully empowered. By aligning with your heart and raising your awareness, you can heal your 'mistakes' (insecurities) before you experience them.

So by moving beyond the polarised view of black and white, we see purpose to all situations and experiences. We also see the power within ourselves to transmute any situation into

Light, enabling all experiences to help us grow. Thus we do not fear any road or path

As we learn to be more confident and ultimately realise that there is nothing to fear, we realise that the world is in fact an exciting place of infinite opportunity with unlimited doors to open and explore.

NEGATION OF OUR OWN INTUITION

Another cause for our indecisions is our incessant negation of our own intuition.

We are constantly told throughout our childhood, adolescence and even adulthood that we must look outside for confirmation of our decisions. Schools, parents, institutions tell us whenever we make a decision to first question it. "Are you sure? What did your boss say? Why have you taken this subject, what are your friends taking? You're too young, I know better". In reality there is no 'better'. There is no right decision. Both are equally valid because both are the choice of the individual. Of course, children require guidance in life, yet to truly learn and be happy they must trust their own decision-making ability. Free will is the ultimate gift, why let another take it away from you?

Remember, if we are constantly seeking validation from others and seeking others to make our decisions for us then we are not truly living. A common example of this is with psychics, psychiatrists and counsellors. For example, psychics are wonderful beings who can offer us insight into the various roads that are open to us. However, we must endeavour not to rely on them to make our choices for us. The same is true for counsellors and psychiatrists. If we are persistently seeing (depending upon) another to choose a path for us or to confirm our decisions, then we are sending a clear message to ourselves that we need others to validate us. We are basically saying that others are more capable of making right decisions in our own lives! This creates an internal theory that we are imperfect in some way as well being weak and needy. These negative beliefs (insecurities) will then be reflected and manifested in all parts of our life.

We already have the answers to all our decisions within. Let us take a very simple example to establish our intuition. Let us say Robert is a gifted and passionate musician who is desperate for a break in the industry. He is offered a two week contract to make a CD that could sell millions or to go on holiday with his friends. What is he going to choose?

Robert will immediately feel compelled to the path that satiates his passion and desire. Sounds too simple, but the real decisions we make are the ones we don't even think about - because we resonate with the response. We intuit. We know.

Making General Decisions

Making decisions can often be time-wasting events as we fret over the possible road to take. Will this road lead me to the Emerald City or it will it take me to the Wicked Witch of the West? Both are perfect! If you 'suffer', you have learned something and are stronger, wiser and ultimately happier. If not, then you have still reached your goal. Dorothy found her way, despite randomly picking paths and getting into trouble. The yellow brick road is your golden path to your dreams, it is already paved! It already has many directions, but they all weave in and out to lead to your Emerald City.

And this is the way to view all decisions. Not simply as one path that serves you and another that does not but to view all paths that serve you! Remember, by viewing everything as pure and perfect, you bring about that perfection into your life.

Let us take an example and look at Angelina. Now Angelina tells herself that she has huge problems making decisions. Every time, she is faced with a decision, she is immediately faced with myriad alternate directions and paths that could possibly lead to a multitude of other directions! However, it is only Angelina that is confusing the situation here! There are a multitude of paths open to you. Always. However, you are not always confused about the direction you choose. Why not? This is because you do not always harbour doubt when making your decision about your path. Angelina feels confused every time she has to make an important decision which affects her life experience. She doesn't want to make the 'wrong' choice.

There are a few lessons here for Angelina to counteract her perpetual indecision. First, she must refrain from distrusting herself for making a 'right' decision. Secondly, she must endeavour to realise that there simply is no right or wrong decision! Thirdly, Angelina may realise that she is harbouring doubt over her ability to handle tough situations. Fourthly is Angelina's obvious attachment to externalities. The last one is crucial because it defines Angelina's perceptions, fears and insecurities - where reliance upon externalities creates dependency and false comfort. She relies upon her external power sources for her security. When she is faced with decisions about a future direction (which all decisions are), these power sources become threatened. And this is what causes Angelina fear and her inevitable indecision.

Angelina's dilemma has never been external; it has always been an internal conflict of belief in herself versus a dis-belief in herself. As you can see there are many factors involved yet by becoming aware of why we do things, we transmute the ignorance within us into wisdom. Awareness is our salvation and our key to ultimate freedom.

When you truly believe in your own power, you will take so-called risks and so-called chances. We have conditioned ourselves for so long to believe that it is too dangerous to plunge ourselves into a pit of variable chance. We've convinced ourselves that it will lead to a negative experience.

So as Angelina learns to empower herself as a Divine being, she sees that she is instead faced with rays of sunshine that all lead to her goal. Angelina realises that each path is blessed, each road vibrantly awaiting her feet to walk upon.

Remember, you are constantly creating! This means that whatever path you choose will not necessarily be the one that you faced when you made your original decision, since other paths will always be merging towards your present intention.

So in this respect, there are no alternate paths once you've made your decision! We tell ourselves, "What if I chose this path instead of that?" However, we are assuming here that our one decision would lead to a definitive result. This is impossible because of the multitude of other decisions we are continually making each and every moment! If your intention is pure within yourself that you intend to follow your heart's desire and ultimately serve yourself, then you attract the benefits from other paths 'that you may have missed'.

We must endeavour to realise that every decision we make, every path we take, is our own sacred choice. As we live our lives with our positive intentions, then all positive benefits will be attracted to our reality anyway! This truth leaves us with the wisdom of knowing that every decision we make is perfect! By harbouring positive intentions, we magnetise and manifest positive experiences into our lives. By embracing the wisdom of perfection in our decisions, we simultaneously brighten, clarify and attract the positive benefits from all other paths to merge with our own.

MAKING DECISIONS CONCERNING OUR SECURITY

To overcome our fear of change, fear of a possible negative future event, we need to target the cause. The cause is a present fear: not knowing from where we are going to draw our power (love). If we make a decision and it leads to an event where we could possibly have nowhere from which to draw power, then this will cause us pain. *This* is ultimately what we fear. Our indecisions in life often result from a fear of losing our power sources, as we attach externally to ensure our happiness.

What is the lesson here? The lesson is to *draw power from within*! This ensures your security. The power (love) within you is far greater than anything you could possibly draw from the outside world. It is infinite!

Let's think about the psychology of this. If we depend upon an externality (such as our partner) for our security/love/power, then we open ourselves to be harmed when that externality changes. When we are fearful of change, we close the doors of possibility because we are latched onto what we presently have. If, on the other hand, we harbour the power within, then we are unmoved by external events. We are fearless of changes to the outside when we know we are secure and happy within. When we are fearless, we are open to more possibilities.

Fear of risk is one of the main instigators of our indecisions. It rides alongside with the fear of change. It is our own fear of displacing our source of security (power/love).

Let us take an example and look at Leanne. Now Leanne is currently in her present job, which she despises! She goes to work, sits at her desk and feels like she would rather be any place else. The work does not challenge her mentally and she feels that if she ever did anything creative in her work it would be cause for a celebration.

Leanne has ideas popping around in her head. She wants to move into a field that is more conducive to her talents, and more importantly, her desires. She dreams for a career in the media.

However, she tells herself that to change her current career and pursue such a notion is in fact a dream. Decisions! What does she do? Does she quit her present job and pursue a dream? Or does she remain in her present job, take the 4 percent pay raise this year and maintain her security?

"I can't quit, I have rent to pay! I have bills to pay!"
"I can't stand my job. My computer is my best friend!"
"My life is so complicated!"

We can see immediately that Leanne has got herself into a condition. She has created so many negative statements that she has lost herself within her own drama. And this is what it is - a drama that she has created. Therefore it is her own creation to change if she desires.

So, we meet with Leanne and we ask her to relax. As she takes a moment and lifts her consciousness out of the situation, Leanne finds herself outside of her drama - her movie. She looks down upon her life and slowly begins to see that she is not in such a predicament. Her life isn't the most complicated thing in the world!

Now, Leanne can see that she has two possible paths (and possibly more)! She is going to examine the two paths to clarify her thoughts. One path allows her to stay within her present job and the other allows her to leave. Neither choice is damned; neither choice is wrong. This is the ultimate realisation. Both are blessed, sacred and perfect because they are her choice. Each is an expression of the Divine.

From this higher perspective, Leanne sees the freedom in seeing the perfection of all choices. Now as she detaches, she may see that she has been allowing her fears to control her decisions or indecisions. The very fact that Leanne has an idea within her that is compelling her towards her dream (in this case the media), is a sign that Leanne wants to pursue that dream! This seems a simple choice. Yet, we almost certainly deny any resonance we feel for a path that frightens us. Our fears will march a crusade in the name of Security! We must endeavour to fight back with our own force of Wisdom, in the name of Love.

Often when we come upon a new path, a new decision, a new route in our lives, we immediately negate it with our fears. Our internal and conditioned fears immediately emerge and tell us that we can't possibly make a right decision! Our fears tell us *"Stop! What are you doing! Are you sure you want to make a change? Any change you make will threaten the status quo and it is the status quo where I know where I am drawing power from!"*

Our fears also claim that we don't know the future so all sorts of things can happen! Yes, we don't know the future, but from where did this philosophy come that says the future outcome is more likely to be negative? This archaic philosophy only limits our world. It limits our doors of possibility and our happiness. Surely this is the opposite of what we want!

Our fears would be happy with the first of everything we come across because immediately it has discovered a source of security. But what happened *before* that source of security? Were we truly damned? Change is the very constant of the Universe! Embrace it!

A man who lives in thirst inside his house will continue to suffer unless he is willing to venture out and take the chance of believing that there is indeed a pond outside. He will persistently tell himself that to venture outside of his house is dangerous. He will tell himself that the rumours of a pond are in fact a mirage that people are fooling themselves into believing is real! However, the moment he steps out of his comfort zone and outside his house (his security) to actually test his theory is the moment he changes his consciousness. He has bypassed his fear and thus transmuted it. He then realises that *there was always water for him to drink*. It was simply his stubborn belief that things could never be kind to him that led to his own suffering.

The point here is not just about the fact that a pond existed near this man. The point is that the man attempted to believe in something his fears persistently told him couldn't be true. Through this belief, this man finds his salvation and ultimate freedom. It is when we challenge things that limit us that we are free.

As we use awareness, we see the illogic of doubt. We understand that to doubt is to enter a field of limitation. It simply serves no one. As soon as we doubt - anything - then we immediately know that we are following the logic and philosophy of a lesser being. To truly appreciate ourselves and the things that are out there for us to accomplish and embrace, we must endeavour to utilise the logic and philosophies of a higher being. These philosophies reflect things that serve us, not attack us - obviously!

CHOOSE TO BELIEVE IN YOURSELF

So, when we are faced with a cross-road of paths, we endeavour to understand what it is we are feeling that is making our indecision so intense. If it is our fear of a probable negative future event, then it is something which states our insecurity in the present. It is something which highlights our attachment to externalities as well as our fear of handling negative situations. Here, we endeavour to look within for our happiness. If you are presently unhappy with a part of your life but feel that to change would cause instability and upset your security, then it is your security that must be questioned. You already have wings to fly if you so choose. We ask ourselves, *"If we take flight, who will cushion us if we fall? Will our wings actually work? Yes, we've seen them work with other people but why should they work with us? Surely something will go wrong!"*

Believe in yourself! Believe in your own capability. Believe in your ability to handle situations. Is this such a hard concept?

Yes. It is hard because you have persistently told yourself (as others have persistently told you), that you are weak, insecure, inferior, or incapable. These all formulate theories within your subconscious mind that you are those things and worse. These theories then affect every thought, decision, action and feeling you have in life.

So, begin by changing the way you approach yourself. See yourself as capable of anything, for if you truly understood the scope of your power you would laugh at your disbelief in yourself. You would instead find it unbelievable that you had any form of doubt over what you could accomplish. You would stop fretting over whether or not you are capable of doing something and instead explore the infinite array of all that you can do. You would realise that the Universe is your oyster, to mould and shape and utilise for your own pleasure. It is you. Children are a prime example here. Being so close to the Divine, they do not fret over decisions they have made or have yet to make because they understand the perfection in all things. And so, they learn and experience happiness at incredible rates.

To counteract our inability to make decisions, we must endeavour to realise this crucial truth: *"Whatever I choose is right!"* There is deep meaning to this. It means that we not only trust the Universe that everything is perfect but we also trust ourselves.

As you realise the perfection in all your decisions, choose paths that serve you! The directions we are led to are the ones we resonate with. They are the directions that leave us feeling freer, more open, creative and happy. The directions or paths that leave us miserable, frustrated and trapped are obviously signs that something is not working! All paths are open to you. Whichever path you take is up to you, they will all lead to your goal if your intent is pure and your decision is aligned with your heart. If you feel good about a decision then you know it is the right one for you. You resonate with the response. If you feel that a decision will leave you freer and take you away from unhappiness then you know that that decision is for you. However, whether you "know" or not is really irrelevant in the end because all paths will merge towards your own as you begin to align yourself more and more with your heart and intentions!

The Universe always serves you because you are the Universe! When you make your choices you become one with all that is around you. You embrace your fundamental birthright as a Creator and you also embrace what you have created before you. For you create for yourself the fork in the road. It is a gift, not a curse! You offer yourself alternate ways of travelling. If indeed another path did serve you slightly better - fear not! That was meant to be and a part of your learning!

You are constantly creating! You are constantly making decisions, whether you realise it or not! Enjoy the ride that is life. It is a free ride and it will twist and turn and loop and barrel. Fear not this ride, for it is a ride of your own, unique calibration. You are not only the train driver but also the passenger. Allow the train to flow with your surroundings and intentions. Travel with your train and allow it to flow onto different tracks or stay on the same one - it is all your choice. But remember one thing: if your intention is pure, the train will reach the same destination, whichever track you are on.

As you make your decisions, know that all results are neutral until you react. It is how you react that defines the decision's polarisation. Are you going to make that experience positive or negative? Raise your vibration even higher and see the compassion in all things; realise the purpose of everything. Everything has purpose of growth; so, whatever the result, it is going to serve you. Everything is meant to be.

Everything is meant to be... This is almost always misunderstood to mean that everything that occurs must be deserved. This is not so! It means that everything is meant to be - everything has purpose. That purpose is growth. So-called 'bad' things that happen to us have purpose of growth, making us happier in the outcome through our learning. So-called 'good' things that occur to us also have purpose of growth, as we enjoy and understand the meaning of happiness.

The lesson here is to realise that all paths are perfect. It is only our own labelling and polarised minds that attempt to box things into right and wrong, good and bad. We attempt to see one path as good and another as bad. Life is not as simple as black and white! *Life is Gold*. It is an endless array of sunshine in all directions. Whichever ray you decide to walk upon, it will always shine beneath your feet and take you to your goals, if you believe in yourself.

This is what the path is all about! It is not about *the path* at all! It is about YOU. It is about how you react to situations and experiences. Whatever comes your way is really irrelevant; it is how you react that defines your experience. Remember the saying, "Life is 10% what you experience and 90% how you react to it."

So, now, do you choose to allow your life experiences to control you or do you control your life experiences? Everything you experience in life is an experience defined by how you choose to experience it!

To truly live in this world is to make decisions. To truly embrace life is to embrace the ultimate gift - the gift of Free Will/ Free Choice. This gift is your Divine birthright allowing you to literally choose what you experience.

There is no 'wrong' inside you. If you see yourself as anything less than Whole and Holy, it is an illusion. You are incapable of fallacy, for you are an expression of the Divine - expanding Universal Consciousness through your magical explorations (choices) in your life. Each choice heralds new opportunity and learning *whatever* the result. Every decision you make is a pure, correct, blessed and divine choice because it has been made by a Sacred Being... You!

You have wings; you always have had and always will. It is up to you to use them or not. THAT is your choice.

Embracing Change

The Universe thrives on change. It is the only constant in reality. When we resist change, we are resisting the very nature of the Universe.

Resistance to change is born out of our fears and insecurities. Our Ego desires stability so that it can harbour its power in an external situation. When we reassess where our power is emanating from and begin to draw our power from within our-Self, we see that external change is not something to be feared.

We are constantly born, die and are reborn in every moment. Our sets of beliefs, opinions, attitudes are constantly changing as we learn – this is the very nature of growth. As we embrace the new, we let go of the old and thus move forward into an arena of unknowingness. It is only when we religiously cling onto what we know that creates disharmony in our lives. The process of spiritual growth can be painful because we are letting go of patterns of thinking that do not want to go! As we die to these outdated modes of thinking, the process of death can be painful, as we enter a new arena of uncertainty and unknowingness. However, as we soon learn that what follows death is a rebirth, we see that we are now awakened with even wider eyes that we had before. Birth is followed by death, which is followed by birth. When we realise the cycle of growth we realise the importance and meaning of this process. By doing so the 'death' process of our beliefs does not become painful as we understand the nature of letting go.

In respect to our lives, we can see that it is essential to embrace change as a crucial part of living. Change is the process of moving forward, it is the process of transcending negativity for it allows us to break free of old patterns. It is only when we resist change that we become stuck in that mode of thinking for however long we choose to remain. Change brings us closer and closer to that state of bliss that we are on the path to achieving.

Our insecurities of change emanate from an innate fear of having something external disrupt our security. The Ego tells us that change can lead to instability and therefore can threaten our state of happiness. However, if this is the case then we know that our state of happiness has been fixed upon an external situation. For example, a change of career might be desperately desired for by an individual. However, that individual's Ego may inform them that change leads to risk - *we do not know what the new career will be like, we do not know what the new people in this career will be like, we do not know whether are capable of doing something different.*

We can begin to see a pattern here and as we raise our awareness we see that we have in fact been giving control of the state of our being to externalities around us. We also realise that our insecurities are based on a fear of risk. We have been for so long conditioned to believe that risk equals instability equals a threat to our happiness. External situations cannot determine your happiness, it is how you react to them that determines this state of being.

If you are open to the very essence of change and begin to see it as an opportunity to learn more and experience more than your abundance will simultaneously bloom. Risk opens us up to the limitless possibilities of abundance, that is already ours to claim. It is only when we ignore change or risk in order to protect that which we know that we block ourselves from generating further happiness. By clinging onto everything that we have and not taking the opportunities that arise, we hinder our growth. We also see the world as a threatening place, one which is out to get us. When in fact we all know deep down that those who enjoy life the most are the ones who embrace change, they fear not the negative things that 'can' happen and embrace the unknowingness that is life.

Change allows us to break free of those old patterns that have been holding us back. Change allows us to bring in new experiences into our lives so that we may have a more expanded view of the world. Ultimately change brings us more happiness and abundance for it is the catalyst for the emergence of new opportunities.

If something is not working in our lives then we should encourage ourselves to make change. It is a sign that we have learned all we can from this experience and are ready to use the wisdom we have so far gained and achieve greater happiness. When we let go of the old and embrace the new, our level of happiness is *always* increasing. This is because we are constantly purifying ourselves of negative thought patterns and limited modes of thinking. Thus we become freer and less afraid with the more change that we allow to affect us.

Fear blinds us to the Truth, it blinds us to opportunities for growth. Fear would have us stay in one place, in one career, with one partner for the whole of our lives. It distracts us from our innate desires to experience new things with its droning rhetoric of how change can lead to danger. This is absurd! Experience new things. If you feel desired to, try out new opportunities. Embrace the limitless possibilities that are awaiting your grasp and you will remember that feeling you had as a child – the eternal knowing that this reality is your playground. The only fear that exists is that which you hold. Let it go and become that which you already are – Spirit in physical form.

If we want to see change in some part of our life, we must first see that part that needs changing in Light. If we see it as something negative, then we will be stuck to it, for negativity binds you to it. For example, if you want to change your career and your present career is mundane and monotonous then send out a prayer request to the Universe of your desire but also see what this present career has been able to teach you. See the gifts that it has given you, for there are gifts in *everything* we do. This present career may have been a lesson to you to change your career! Sometimes we push ourselves into explicitly monotonous work to give us a spiritual kick up the backside to show us that there are other paths should we dare to take them. We can say to ourselves, "My present career has given me great insight into revealing to me that I feel I can do something creative. By experiencing this current work, it has given me an extra incentive to go out and do something that I really want to do now."

Let's take an example: a man may have been diligently searching for a high-flying career in a City bank over the past year but still to no avail. Now this man may actually do very well in his career, however if he looks at his reasons for his search he may realise that it might not fully align with his highest intentions. There are of course many people who are aligned in this course and work very well and happily in City banks, however let us say for argument that for this man his true vocation has always been in architecture. He may desire this banking job in the City due to cultural conditioning or peer pressure from his friends. So he may now look at his true reasons and see that it has been driven to gain some kind of power through the money and status aspect that this kind of job seems to provide. He may hold the belief that once he attains this position he will be happy. It is as soon as we come to that line of thinking where we believe that an external event will bring us the happiness we so desire that we know that we are missing something in our lives. We know that we are chasing something that can never be. We are placing our entire happiness in something outside of us , which is always subject to change.

In this example, this man may realise that he has been denying himself from pursuing a job in a field that he may have always wanted to do in architecture. When he finally aligns himself with that inner desire of what he always wanted to do, he realises that he is happy *just* by pursuing this dream. This of course will attract more and more abundance as he is not only aligning himself with his inherent talents as an architect but he is also allowing himself to be happy in the Now, free of externalities. He empowers the belief within his subconscious mind that he is happy, therefore manifesting and attracting greater happiness towards him.

When we break down our pursuits and actions in this world we see a wonderful myriad of our loves, intentions and desires as well as our fears and insecurities. We can effectively see how the Ego part of ourselves is interfering in our decisions and thought processes and ultimately break free of them. Awareness is the key to all forms of freedom. The simple awareness of why we are really doing something, immediately begins the process of releasing and purifying ourselves to align with our deepest Truths. The more we stray from our highest intentions and inner feelings, the more unhappy we become. Yet so many of us do this so much of the time!

Of course, many will feel that they cannot break out of certain commitments that they have. However, it is the very act of opening your awareness to what you truly desire and believing that you *can* achieve that dream that will bring that ambition closer to you. We tend to use the word "trapped" or "can't" when we describe our lives and use commitments to describe how we cannot take a risk to pursue such 'radical' dreams. However, there is always something deeper to these fears than the Ego will let on. Fear of taking risk is based on a fear of rejection, a fear of possible failure by stepping outside the box of societal norm. Our Ego will jump up and down if such a suggestion props up of doing something 'out of the norm', because it knows that security is under threat and it will use any excuse to bring you back inside the pen of normal behaviour. However, these fears of rejection, failure and risk are blockages to what we can all achieve, they are simply fears and have no real basis. When we feel something and feel an urge to do something and take a risk, life will accommodate us towards these ends.

Think back on the risks that you have taken that you have felt an urge to do – providing you are doing this out of a love for this dream and not out of fear, they will have all worked out. This is because fear has no purpose and no foundation in any kind of logic - be it spiritual or traditional. We are each designed *specifically* to achieve our inner desires and our inner dreams. In fact it is stranger when we don't align with these dreams! There is something that you can do that no other is capable of. It is your unique gift to the world and it is your Divine birthright to claim and utilise it to its limit. When we take a risk, we are ultimately expressing our faith. When we express our faith, we are surrendering to the eternal NOW, we are letting go of our expectations and beliefs. This is what faith really is, it is the ability to let go of all attachments especially expectations.

You are the prison guard to your own prison! You have the key to let yourself free if you dare to trust that it is you that has this power. You have always had the key, you have just long been led to believe that it is others that control your freedom.

Know that when things in your life are right you will know that they are right because they will come with ease. Nature thrives on *effortlessness* and this is a fundamental spiritual principle. When you are at ease, you are allowing. This allowing gives you unprecedented access to abundance because it is an act of flowing with the energy of the Universe. When you are at ease with yourself you are creating ease in your reality. The outdated mode of thinking whereby hard work and sacrifice will reward you with the things you desire *is outdated*! Things that you desire come through ease.

GOING WITH THE FLOW

The Universe is your oyster. It is your playground to play in. There are no rules on who deserves this or that, you deserve anything you desire – and you have been given the free will to take it as you choose. You do not need to compete for another's share of abundance, there is enough to go round for everybody. We have simply forgotten how the whole system works. When we resist the flow of energy in the Universe, we create blockages and blockages are not healthy. If we resist something in our reality and see it as an obstacle and try to ignore it then we are creating a blockage – and we are forgetting the fact that we have created this 'obstacle' in our path in the first place! So in reality we are resisting our-Self.

The Universe is much like a living organism (on a much grander scale of course) and by relating it to ourselves we can understand better how it works. When we resist things in our life, we are stopping the circulation of energy (blood) through the Universe – and this creates dis-ease. By being at ease with all things that happen we allow them to pass and not to build up and cause us pain. The more we focus on what we do not want, the more it will remain in our lives. This is because we feed this situation with our energy and it unwittingly attracts more of the same. The key is to focus on something else, detach our emotions from the situation and turn our attention elsewhere.

Occasionally, we find ourselves in situations where we feel that nothing is happening. We feel that we have tried so hard to make a change or manifest something in our lives but nothing is occurring. For Lightworkers this can be tremendously frustrating for you are geared to learn and grow at phenomenal speeds! Here it can be fitting to accept that this 'Timeout' is part of our growth. There are times when to release blockages, our Higher Selves move us into positions where we are made to 'stop' and see for a moment, who we really are. When we are constantly flittering and fluttering around, reading this book and talking to that person, we sometimes forget who *we* really are. Spiritual growth at this time is all about working on your-Self, it is about finding who you really are. So here again, it is more fitting for us to go with the flow that there is no flow!

We can look at Dolphins as a wonderful example of how to *allow*. Dolphins swim effortlessly with or against the current of the ocean. Their sleek, serene bodies do not attach to anything in the ocean and they glide graciously through the ocean in joy. Dolphins show us a way of swimming through life in such majesty and tranquillity. When we let go of our attachments and expectations we release ourSelves into the eternal ocean of existence. There is no worry or judgement or need to be in anything apart from the truth of one Self.

Life is energy, like the ocean. It is only when we resist the energy or hold on to it that it causes us pain. When we experience the energy, simultaneously letting go, we are on the ride of a lifetime. We are swimming with grace and splendour. We are at peace. Here we can learn to go with the flow in any area of our life. Always return to the knowingness of I AM. It is totality.

Embracing Tumultuous Change Through Detachment

"No matter how long the night, the day is sure to come."
- Congo proverb

When we experience periods in our life, where our world seems to fall apart or break down, it is important for us to realise the necessity of such situations as part of our growth. When a storm rages, seemingly devastating all in its path, it is the serenity of calm that it leaves in its wake. Similarly, it is important for us to experience such emotional turbulence in our lives, for us to clear away old patterns and achieve a stillness within us.

Of course, dealing with the storms in our lives can be the most difficult things we ever do. However, it is here where we can use an element of detachment so that we do not get caught up in the power of the storm, thereby forgetting its true purpose. It is when we resist the storm and attempt to shield ourselves from its inevitability that we prolong the turbulent experiences in our lives.

There is a cycle to all things – birth, death, rebirth. It is the nature of nature! By detaching ourselves from a particularly distressing situation in our lives, where things seem to be falling apart, we can actually speed up the process and bring in that serenity that we so desire. As we acknowledge the need and purpose of the chaos in our lives as an important part of the 'death' process of our insecurities and old patterns, we are reborn. We take flight into a world where we have worked through those issues and that particular storm will not return.

Emotional detachment can be very difficult. However, it is born first out of the realisation of why it is better for us to detach. This is of course, realising that we will be happier in the outcome. Once we realise and acknowledge this, we can lift ourselves up out of the storm and view it from above. We can see the lessons to be learned but ultimately we see the nature of the storm and its true purpose. The storm, like death, is integral to our existence.

When we embrace and allow our chaotic experiences as being part of a higher purpose for ourselves to grow from, then we are one step closer to creating harmony in our lives. As we deal with all the parts of ourselves that give rise to the storm, then eventually the storms will have no fuel to ignite. We will have attained a state of tranquillity.

Asking for Help

Do not be afraid to ask for help if you are vulnerable. Acting strong in a situation when we are in pain only creates more separateness and causes more pain. Life is about co-creating and sharing. When we are open to receive love, then we become more open to give love – and vice versa.

We all go through pain just as anybody else. Understand that you are going through pain for some reason but also understand that by sharing with another you can get their perspective. This is because we often become too attached to our emotions which cloud our perception of what the pain is trying to teach us. As a Lightworker, you can set an example to others by expressing yourself in moments of pain and revealing the wisdom behind it, creating waves of openness in those around you. People will follow in your footsteps and begin to share with others too, divulging your innate wisdom.

Some of us can be very stubborn when it comes to sharing feelings! Many take pride in their statements that they do not need to share their feelings or be open about them. It is a cultural belief not to reveal your vulnerability in fear of it making you look weak. However, true courage comes from those who are fearless of breaking cultural traditions and wish to evolve. The bravest thing is to accept that you are experiencing painful situations and are willing to face them head on. By cowering away from your painful feelings only allows them to fester, grow and control you in other parts of your life.

Whilst pride may seem admirable, it can limit your abundance. This is because pride is just a block to greater freedom. We like to do things on our own and often don't like asking for help because others may view us as weak or incapable of doing something on our own. At the end of the day, others do not care! They have their own realities to think about. Do you honestly look at those who ask for help with contempt? Do you honestly look down upon them? If anything we admire those who have the courage to ask for help because they grow and change exponentially.

When we ask for help we are sending a clear message to our subconscious mind and the Universe – we are saying that we are not resisting the flow of energy and we are willing to give *and* receive. This is terribly important, because if we are not willing to receive then we are creating a block in the circulation of energy and the Universe will respond by not giving.

Unconditional Receiving

Each moment you are changing. The person you were a year ago is different than the one you are now, just as the person you will be in a year will be different to the one that you are now. All that really matters is who you are NOW, for that determines both the present and the future.

When we cling onto things in your life, we find ourselves being hurt. A need for security arises from our deep insecurities of change. Fear of change, fear that what we have may not last, fear of scarcity – this is because we are seeking power from external sources. When we are happy in the love that we have ourselves, then any change that occurs on the outside can never affect this state of being. Resisting things in our life is resisting the flow of energy in the Universe. It is pointless fighting things that we have created! For we are only fighting ourselves!

By unconditionally receiving, we are embracing all things that come into our lives because we fundamentally realise that we are the ones that have created it to be so. We are taking responsibility for our creations, sending a powerful message to our subconscious mind that we are acknowledging the power within us. The subconscious mind reacts accordingly and sets into motion a stronger belief that we are indeed powerful creators.

Unconditional receiving allows us to see an obstacle become a challenge and the challenge becoming part of our growth making us stronger and wiser beings of light. When we constantly fight the Universe and blame it for our challenges then it will only lead to more challenges, for we are in reality fighting ourselves. When we dislike what we see in our lives and long for future change, we distance ourselves from this ever becoming a reality! By loving all that we create, we allow our subconscious mind to believe that we indeed love ourselves (our creations), which will then be reflected in our outer reality.

Be ready to receive anything that comes your way with Love. When you allow for the flow of energy to pass through you and not become attached to everything, you send a clear signal to your subconscious that you are a master of your destiny.

Here you send out a clear message that you accept that everything before you is a result of your own manifestation on account of your own thoughts. By saying "OK, I created this, I will deal with it" you reiterate to yourself that you do indeed create your reality and you move into a conscious arena of creating exactly what you desire in your life.

Ultimately Unconditional Receiving allows us to embrace the Magic that is always around us, in every step we make, in every breath we take. This Universe is a cosmic Magician playing untold tricks to itself, forever in mystery and forever in joy at its own experience of its mysteriousness. Enjoy the mystery, magicians

Unconditional Acceptance

Unconditional Acceptance is the Truth that all things are meant to be. Once you accept this fundamental principle your world grows exponentially as there is more room for infinite expansion. Every decision you make and every situation you encounter is Perfection. This is because it is based on the Law of Free Will and the underlying essence of the Universe - Love. If the situation breeds a perceived mistake, we see the lesson to be learned and we are one step closer to revealing the GOD within. If the situation breeds happiness then we are experiencing Love. Both lead to our inner GOD. It is only when we resist our reality, thereby resisting the flow of energy in our world that we encounter resistance in response from the Universe.

When we attempt to resist a manifestation in our reality as we try to shy away from something in our world or ignore it, then we are telling our subconscious that we are not responsible for what lies before us. Therefore we will find it extremely difficult to consciously manifest our true desires.

When we accept and receive all that comes our way with grace and valour then we inform ourselves that we know we are the Master Creator of our reality, so let us now move into *consciously* creating our reality.

Accept that you do not hold the answers to everything. Such a statement means that anything can happen. Yes, anything can happen! Yet this is nothing to be fearful of. This is something to rejoice about, for it is the prospect of unpredictability that makes life so interesting and exciting.

HUMILITY

When you live in gratitude you appreciate everything that you have – and what you appreciate, appreciates even more.

See yourself as the child on a beach, looking up at the stars, the heavens, the higher realms. There are worlds upon worlds out there, beings upon beings, galaxies upon galaxies.

Each of you has an army of spiritual guides, angels, and helpers *just for You*. You each have constant attention focused on you. Whether you are asleep or awake, there are countless beings working non-stop to guide and assist you and send their ever radiant love. You are *never* alone, no matter how much you believe yourself to be. Also know that the GOD is always with you, for He/She *IS* you. Whatever you experience, GOD experiences, whenever you are alone, GOD is alone with you. Therefore you are *never* alone!

Today, thank the universe for all the things that you subconsciously take for granted. The food you eat – how did it get all the way to your mouth? There was a lot of work involved in that on the part of your many of brothers and sisters. The pure beauty of nature that you see before your eyes – thank Gaia for her un-blemishing devotion to humanity. The plants that give you the oxygen to breathe. Thank the Universe for being able to thank the Universe! You are alive, you exist and you are All That Is.

Humbleness will increase you power through your acknowledgment of the power of the Universe. When you are humble, you are in a state of wide-eyed wonder, eternally grateful for everything around you. This is a profound concept. For you are loving all things, without any influence of power, of the Ego. You are magically entranced by the wonders of the Universe and your place in it.

However, humility is not about power and that is its power! Humility is about the divine wonder of creation, the sacred submission to the magnitude of all that exists around us. Recognising our wonderful powerful place within it simultaneously our small part within such a grand complex system that is working together in ways that we will eternally work to understand.

Prayer of Gratitude

I thank the whole of Creation for Being and allowing me to Be, for Giving and allowing me to Give, for Loving and allowing me to Love. I am eternally grateful.

JOY, PASSION, PLAYFULNESS

Feel the burning desire within you, for it is the fire of your soul – the ever-burning radiance of your Inner Child, who never gets tired or bored. Let your Child out to experience the wonder of this world with all the awe and marvel of an innocent.

'Being spiritual' is not just about sitting back and being still. It can very well be, and this is can be tremendously peaceful and serene but it is also about letting loose the passion within you. And letting it loose onto the world, for it will provide a catalyst for all those around you to wake up.

We are playing a Game that we have created to experience the richness and fullness of creation. So let us enjoy the journey.

Life is not meant to be about tests and should's and shouldn'ts, it is about the realisation that you can live in pure joy and bliss. In fact release the words "should" and "shouldn't" from your vocabulary! It serves no one anyone good. Learning does not have to be serious as institutional schools have persistently drilled into us. Learning is about enjoying the experience of growth. To learn is to acquire knowledge to become wiser; and with wisdom comes greater awareness and ultimately greater happiness. When one is serious, they view the world through the eyes of judgement – where if they misalign themselves with a particular goal, they feel they have done something wrong. This is more duality consciousness!

Having passion for something can serve everything, including yourself. Passion gives you the drive and excitement to follow your dreams and doesn't punish you for perceived mistakes. Instead, it sees them as more learning and interesting challenges. Through passion we can truly en-joy our experiences. Many of us have fallen asleep in our lives - going to school, university, getting our 9-5 jobs, house, mortgage – and we believe that a holiday once a year might be asking too much sometimes!

You have a passion for something that you truly love doing. Discover what that passion is. You will immediately know what it is because you will feel like it isn't work (in the traditional sense). There is an effortlessness is pursuing your heart's desire. This is because it resonates with your inner being and is completely natural to you. You will feel like you could do it forever and no matter how little money you had, you would still do this work. Locate that passion, for that is where your unique skills lie. Remember passions can change and allow them to change, for you have more unique skills and talents than you could possibly realise. You are also adapting to new things for we learn and assimilate at tremendous speeds. You are the eternal explorers of consciousness and love to learn.

There is something you can give that *no* other can. Find that unique gift and immerse your-Self in it.

Remember that is important to live in joy, for this is the reason that you are here – to realise that life can be lived in joy as opposed to pain and suffering. Ignore the illusion that tells you that you must suffer and sacrifice to balance the rewards in life. You *already* deserve all the happiness that you can imagine, and more!

Life is about play. We have for so long been led to believe that life is an endurance, almost like a prison sentence where we do as much as we can to survive. This is simply not the case, you have always been the prison keeper to your own prison. You hold the keys to our freedom. And freedom comes through the realisation of joy, the acceptance that you are allowed to be happy and can be happy *whenever* you choose.

Look back on the past six months and see how much you have grown. You are growing at tremendous rates that is breaking all records. Look less at those around you for "spiritual competition" or as a base to see how much you have grown. You all have your unique path and what may energise you may not another. We all have our individual lessons at various times on our journey. Remember, this is not a race! Because the race has already been won! This is about our-Selves. This is about how you can truly work on your-Self. We so often chastise ourselves for not moving forward or for taking so long to learn a particular lesson. Remember, that there really is no one that judges you apart from your-Self. Sometimes, when we seem to be stuck, we are growing the most – for we are assimilating and assessing our actions on a much grander spiritual level.

Take time to return to the eternal knowingness of existence – the totality of NOW. Here you can bring in the joy that we all desire in our lives. It is important to keep the balance of work and play in our lives. Many of us treat spiritual work as very serious, however in time we will see that this too can be worked on through play. Living in joy is living in constant joy *all* the time. There is en-joy-ment to be born out of every situation.

Living in Flow
Letting Go of Control & Surrendering to All That Is

We live our lives as a feather, blowing in the wind, desperately trying to work out where the feather will land or control which direction it will take. In truth, we never know where our feather takes us – and this is a beautiful thing – to allow the feather to breeze through existence with eternal freedom and infinite possibility.

If we look at our lives, we see that there may be control everywhere. We attempt to control our thoughts, our actions, our perceptions, our futures, our emotions, the people around us, our careers, our behaviours. It is all a reflection of a philosophy based in fear, where we assume that control equates to security. We assume that if I know the result of this series of actions then I will be safe. If I know what this person is thinking I will be safe. If I know why all this is happening to me right now then I will be safe. If I know what I will be doing in 3 months time I will be safe.

The paradox of control is that all it does is generate more insecurity! For as we continually look externally for our security – the future, other people, facts – we are continually at the whim of the external world – which is always changing. We are also basing our future expectations on past experiences, limiting our future experiences! Because it does not open us up to new experiences, ones we have never experienced before. We can never know what we will be doing in 3 months time. We do not know the reasons behind all the things that happen to us right now. It is our fears of the unknown that drive us towards creating a pretence that will satiate us in the here and now.

When we surrender, we let go of Everything – we are in a state of pure Trust. This is a place of pure potentiality, pure expectancy. It is a place of unknowingness and herein lies our freedom.

For when we are present in this state of uncertainty and unknowingness then we are allowing ourselves to experience life at its utmost. We are open to *all* possibilities. We are not resisting anything.

There are many times in our lives where we reach a point of pure despair. The path towards this point of hopelessness is littered with many challenges that we have perceived as obstacles and many attachments that we are too emotionally involved with. Yet it is often when we reach a point of despair that we totally surrender – we give up our incessant need for attachments and finally relinquish our desperate need to control everything in our lives. It is this point of surrender where we unconditionally accept everything in our lives instead of fighting. And so we are allowing the circulation of energy in the Universe to flow. Then we find as soon as we surrender, we have been given what we have desired.

There is of course a fine line here since we do not need to reach a point of despair to achieve our goals and aspirations! This is merely an opportunity for us to understand *why* such a point of desolation can lead to our salvation. For when we surrender all that we have, we are issuing a powerful statement to the Universe, saying, "I surrender all my attachments. I have nothing and so nothing can harm me. I no longer give my power to that which is external to me and that which I have been trying to control. I am free from it all"

Wisdom is the knowledge that true happiness doesn't come from knowledge! It is the total surrender to the unknowingness. It is the trust that within the unknowingness lies infinite creativity, abundance and excitement. Excitement is born out of a surrender to the unknowingness. When you are excited you are in a state of positive expectancy of things that you do not know! You are like a child, eyes open wide gazing into the heavens, uncontrollably amazed that such wonders exist. There are no expectations, attachments or need for knowing – you are experiencing.

Experiencing comes from surrendering to the moment, allowing all things to be, allowing for the Universe to circulate all energy, the knowing that all things are interconnected and meant to be. Each moment you are reborn as infinite potential, you are totally surrendering yourself to a greater Divine Plan that we are all experiencing together.

When you realise that the Universe has your best intentions at heart *always*, you reach a place of such peaceful serenity that you can totally let go. And herein lies true freedom. Faith is the total trust in the Universe within – the total trust that *everything* is available to you. It is also the total trust that *all* things are meant to be. *All things*. It is the knowing that within all experiences lies purpose – be it a purpose of gaining wisdom or a purpose in attaining joy. When you totally surrender to this knowing, *anything* is possible.

When you surrender yourself to the Universe, you are issuing the most profound of all statements. You are saying "I trust where I am. I trust where I have been and I trust where you will take me". Through this we attract incredible abundance and incredible profound miracles that are leading us to greater freedom and ultimately back to our true state as Supreme Creators.

Surrender dissolves all those links and attachments you form with so many things that control your happiness. Surrender is the ultimate source of freedom while simultaneously being the ultimate way of magnetising abundance and miracles.

When we surrender and release all that we hold so dearly to ourselves, then we are truly free to receive the innate guidance from Source that is so ready to give. We can only truly hear what this guidance has to offer us when we let go of all our attachments, to everything and sink deep within ourselves to what has always existed and what truly exists and will always exist – Source.

When you surrender and release, you connect with Source at your deepest level and you hear what the Universe has to say to you. This allows you to totally surrender to the moment. You totally surrender to the eternal interconnectedness of all things. It is a total allowance of *everything* as well as a total allowance of who you are.

SO HOW DO WE LIVE IN THE FLOW?

Living in Flow requires us to take each moment as it comes and BE within it. What are we feeling? What are we feeling right now? This is the most important aspect of being – it is our emotions. Is it happiness, is it anger, is it joy, is it fear? And we look from our non-polarised eyes and see it without judgement. We do not label it, we recognise that all emotions are pure. All of them deserve the attention and expression as any other emotion. And we practice this with whatever emerges. Because it is within these emotions that we are given our divine guidance. Consequently we are allowed to grow at remarkable rates because we are doing all that our soul is asking – to release what is flowing through.

Remember, your emotions are flowing through! Emotions, or e-motion, is energy-in-motion. It requires movement, it lives in movement. When we are not allowing our beautiful divine emotions to flow through us, we are denying a part of ourselves and causing that energy to block in a various aspects of ourselves. This then like any blockage causes us suffering in our lives.

Another step is for us to allow for everything in our current reality. For when we allow for what is currently occurring, we accept ourselves as the Creators of what is occurring. We also allow the energies to flow because it is important for us to remember there is the whole of existence involved in this Creation. We allow, and energy moves and we move on to the next experience. Remembering that each experience is divinely meaningful, which we can use for our growth.

One of the key aspects of living in the flow of life is to have faith in the process. The process is the Universe! To be in flow is to trust that all things have their divine meaning. This is not simply hope, for hope is anticipation mired with doubt.

Faith is to be naked in the knowing that you will be clothed. It is the faith that there is a complexity to life that is beyond our current understanding. It is the knowing that the unknown is a place of true safety, contradicting what our fears (and our societies, reflecting or fears) have taught us. Faith can be the process of surrendering rigid fixations on having to know why or how things work and accepting the fact that we are on a learning path. Therefore we do not need to know how everything works! Our fears cannot accept the unknown because the unknown represents in-security and instability. However, it is from this unknown where miracles are born. It is the complete surrender to faith that we open to the deepest truths of the Universe. For we have no expectations, needs, attachments – we know instead that we are part of something magical. It is that knowing that frees us into accessing it.

As we release our emotions we also look at each moment as powerful signs. When we surrender to the moment, we dissolve all expectations and attachments, we embrace our natural state. In that sacred moment we become at One with the entire Cosmos. And it is in this holy instant that we are fully open to all the Divine guidance and loving miracles that are always available.

DIVINE GUIDANCE

Divine guidance is speaking to us constantly, every moment of our lives. The Universe speaks to us in gentle whispers, never wishing to infringe on our sacred free will. When we surrender to each moment and see each as perfect, we let go of our mind's control of our reality – in other words the constant revision of past events and future ones. Instead we become truly focused on what is happening in our space right now. We see each event as highly purposeful and meaningful, we direct our energies here and now. We listen, we feel, we acknowledge our current emotions and give them validation. We release and express. Divine wisdom flows from our hearts. It flows through our being. Our hearts are continually singing our unique notes into the Universe, merging with other notes to become the chorus of Creation. This Creation is what we are experiencing. This note exists in the eternal present moment. The more we are here, in this moment, the more we can recognise, feel and resonate with the sound of our note – and follow its divine guidance.

And as we flow we begin to tap into the magic of the Universe, where by living in a state of surrender and humility, we allow for synchronicity to become a true force in our lives.

Synchronicity is testament to our surrendering. Here we see each moment of existence as immeasurably purposeful. Each moment signposting us to our next stage of excitement. How do we look for the signs? It is when we acknowledge the small signs that the big signs emerge – because in truth, every single aspect of our reality is a sign! For all is a reflection of the Universe within. As we live and experience and meet others, our heart will pick up and resonate an emotion. Our heart speaks in a simple gentle voice – so gentle, never pushing, just asking yourself "Are we living in love?"

Each moment our heart is speaking about something that it resonates with - "this would interest us", "I feel connected to this person", "I like what that person said", "writing this makes me feel connected". When we listen to our heart and follow it, incredible miracles occur – for that is what they are – miracles. Profound sacred moments that we honour for the whole of creation has been involved in bringing it to us! Following these signs, lead us to greater opportunities that serve us.

To follow our heart, we surrender to the magnificence of creation, we surrender to each moment – understanding that we create our own reality and we have created all of this. We do not need to intentionally control our creations, we are here to live in the mystery of life, we are here to enjoy. If we have trouble with what to do or where to go, we only need to look at the majestic teachers entering our plane on a daily level. Children are our teachers for living in flow. They bring that knowledge, wisdom and ultimately – being.

Spiritual Human Being

It is being that allows us to live in the flow. Being. Being with every emotion that flows through us now. Being with every action and interaction that is occurring to us now. Being with everything around us now. And Being with all of it without judgment, coming from Love. When we are in a state of being, we are in true joy – for we are recognising that life has literally just been born. We have just been born into this moment, where yet again a new Universe has been born for us to experience.

You may be feeling an emotion related to a past event, yet if you are feeling it now, honour it. Express it. Release it. Releasing can come in many forms, writing, expressing to another, drama, exercise. As long as we acknowledge the emotion for what it is and allow it to flow.

Remember the Universe is constantly guiding you towards your highest goals and purpose – constantly! That is the only way the Universe can work! The Universe is not against you, it is gently showing the way. It is you! When something is blocking in our lives, it is a clear sign it is not working. How do we know? We know because our internal barometer – our emotions – will let us know. We feel stuck, we feel trapped, we feel like we are trying everything and nothing is happening. The message is so clear – try a new way, find a new path. Yet we spend so much of our energies trying to channel our feather down a particular passageway! Our higher aspect realises that this passageway may lead to a dead-end around the corner – yet we cannot see this from our perspective. Simultaneously our higher aspect may see other roads leading to wondrous joy that we cannot currently see on the ground level.

Of course our emotions are also signs of aspects of ourselves that require healing, so how do we know the difference between a closed path and one that we are meant to overcome? We know by surrendering to what is happening now. We treat the now as all that exists, for that is the truth! We embrace and release the emotions associated with this current situation and that is where the healing occurs. We will then see paths clear or continue to be blocked, ushering us to find alternate paths.

Accept that you do not hold the answers to everything. This is OK! Wherever you are, whatever you are doing is perfect. How do we know that? Because you have created it! That alone is acknowledgement of its perfection. You are a perfect being, reflecting that perfection into the world around you. You are experiencing perfection and the universe is experiencing it through you.

The Universe is You. When you surrender to the Universe, you are surrendering to yourself! You are All That Is. You are all creation. The conscious aspect of you here may not know what is going to happen, yet the Higher aspect of you holds all possibilities. However, the beauty of this plane is that we do not know what is going to happen! Thus we birth pure potentiality and possibility. You are capable of anything, any possible outcome –

and all, every single path your chose will result in your happiness. For a seemingly negative experience will bring you greater wisdom to increase your happiness for all future moments, a positive experience will bring you happiness in that moment.

There are hundreds of billions of stars in this galaxy, billions of galaxies in this universe and no doubt many universes and realms beyond what we know. This gives us a dual perspective. On one level we are deeply humbled by the beauty of eternity, we are a part of a Grand Scheme of Existence that is playing out on a level totally beyond our comprehension. Feel the awesomeness of your surroundings for a moment. Breathe it in and surrender to the magnificence. On another level, we are part of this Grand Scheme of Existence! You are All That Is – you are All of This. This Greater Consciousness is with your every breath, your every action, nothing goes unnoticed by All That is.

Do you realise how special you are? You are an integral part of this entire cosmos – watched with a love beyond comprehension. When we surrender to All That Is, we realise that there are many other aspects involved in our lives than our conscious aspects on the grounded level of Earth reality can comprehend. We are the instruments of Love, playing our notes across creation for purposes beyond our understanding. Our resonance travelling into this infinite eternity affecting everything in its path. And we do not need to understand it!

When we have faith and trust in the beautiful scheme, we release all worry, doubt, fear and sink into the same knowingness that all children are born with – that life is a wonder to cherish and to play within. Each moment born a new world. Each moment born a new paradise for us to create within. Each moment serving us.

Become the feather in your life. Float on the winds of the Universe, knowing that the Universe is taking you into the unknown. Surrender to the unknown and the infinite possibilities that are within your grasp. Feel the eternal safety that you are always cared for by the Great Cosmos, always guided and always unconditionally loved for everything you say, do, think and feel.

You are an Infinite Being.

About the author

Vaz Sriharan

Vaz is a channel writer, clairsentient and spiritual activist living in London, England. Vaz experienced severe depression for approximately 15 years. Exploring many diverse spiritual texts and his own connection, Vaz accessed profound wisdoms in 2003 when he was 24 years old. During this time, the information channelled assisted Vaz into recognising that he was able to experience anything he wanted, by using certain revolutionary techniques of blending spiritual truths with modern psychology.

In 2007, Vaz founded the London College of Spirituality, a grassroots movement designed to help awaken Londoners for the shift. This organisation accumulated 4,000 members in 4 years and is committed towards the empowerment of humanity through principles of Truth, Integrity and living the message of Unconditional Love Vaz believes that grassroots empowerment leads to collective harmony.

Vaz is involved in social work and actively encouraging the greater accessibility of spiritual truths. He is committed towards empowering individuals and allowing them to have the ability to use truths to better their lives. "Freedom is within our grasp, we just have to know it's there and where to look".

To see more about Vaz's work, please visit *www.warriorsoflove.com* and *www.londoncollegeofspirituality.co.uk*

About London College of Spirituality

The London College of Spirituality (LCS) is a grassroots social enterprise, a portal for infinite individuals, You, to share, explore and connect with others on a similar wavelength - an open one.

LCS has a vision to see humanity awakened - a world where each individual realises their innate inner power, untapped abilities and limitless potential, evolving collectively through the ideology of unconditional love. LCS works to hold a space for individuals to discover themselves through talks, social events, healing nights, classes, workshops and events.

LCS is involved in many social issues and committed towards the development of sustainable communities that work with the planet.

Events at LCS are run at very low costs to encourage the accessibility of spiritual truths. If you would like to donate towards LCS or towards this book, and the greater work that is being done, please visit www.londoncollegeofspirituality.co.uk for more information

Blessings on your journey beautiful soul.

Acknowledgments

To the Great Spirit, One Source, Boundless Love that gives endlessly. For watching, loving and showing me the way, always finding ways to show me my light when I was too lost to see. To Gaia for leading me across lands and seas to find myself all over the world.
Sri, Savitri, Meera, Anjela, Andie, Aang, Carly, Lila, Candine, Ross, Inken, Catherine, Sunil. All those on my journey reflecting who I am back to me in all ways, supported me, and all those involved in this divine game.

The Illumination of One Candle, illuminates the surroundings for a thousand others...to discover the illumination within themselves